HUGH BUNCH WARMS HIMSELF IN HIS CENTURY-OLD GENERAL STORE IN KINGSTON, ARKANSAS.

America's Hidden

Prepared by the Special Publications Division
National Geographic Society, Washington, D. C.

YOUNG COUPLE FINDS SECLUSION BESIDE DEER LAKE ON MICHIGAN'S UPPER PENINSULA.

Corners

Places Off the Beaten Path

LOWELL GEORGIA

PRAIRIE DOG POPS OUT OF ITS BURROW IN SOUTH DAKOTA'S WIND CAVE NATIONAL PARK.

AMERICA'S HIDDEN CORNERS

Contributing Authors: LESLIE ALLEN,
  MARY ANN HARRELL, CHRISTINE ECKSTROM LEE,
  H. ROBERT MORRISON, THOMAS O'NEILL,
  GENE S. STUART, SUZANNE VENINO

Contributing Photographers: NATHAN BENN,
  MATT BRADLEY, JIM BRANDENBURG, PAUL CHESLEY,
  DAN DRY, LOWELL GEORGIA, ANNIE GRIFFITHS

Published by The National Geographic Society
GILBERT M. GROSVENOR, *President*
MELVIN M. PAYNE, *Chairman of the Board*
OWEN R. ANDERSON, *Executive Vice President*
ROBERT L. BREEDEN, *Vice President, Publications and
  Educational Media*

Prepared by The Special Publications Division
DONALD J. CRUMP, *Editor*
PHILIP B. SILCOTT, *Associate Editor*
WILLIAM L. ALLEN, WILLIAM R. GRAY, *Senior Editors*

Staff for this book
PAUL D. MARTIN, *Managing Editor*
JOHN G. AGNONE, *Picture Editor*
JODY BOLT, *Art Director*
MONIQUE F. EINHORN, PATRICIA F. FRAKES, *Researchers;*
  PALMER GRAHAM, BARBARA GRAZZINI, *Assistant Researchers*
LESLIE ALLEN, MARY ANN HARRELL,
  CHRISTINE ECKSTROM LEE, H. ROBERT MORRISON,
  LISA A. OLSON, GENE S. STUART, JENNIFER C. URQUHART,
  SUZANNE VENINO, *Picture Legend Writers*
JOHN D. GARST, JR., PATRICIA K. CANTLAY,
  ROBERT E. DULLI, *Map Research and Production*
REBECCA B. JOHNS, CAROL A. ROCHELEAU,
  Illustrations Assistants

Engraving, Printing, and Product Manufacture
ROBERT W. MESSER, *Manager*
GEORGE V. WHITE, *Production Manager*
GREGORY STORER, *Production Project Manager*

Foreword   6

The Great Basin   8

The Chesapeake Bay   34

The Prairie and Badlands   62

The Upper Peninsula   92

The Gulf Coast   116

The Ozarks   144

The Four Corners   170

Notes on Contributors   196

Acknowledgments   196

Index   197

MARK R. DUNLEVY, RICHARD A. McCLURE,
  DAVID V. SHOWERS, *Assistant Production Managers;*
  MARY A. BENNETT, *Production Assistant;*
  JULIA F. WARNER, *Production Staff Assistant*
NANCY F. BERRY, PAMELA A. BLACK,
  MARY FRANCES BRENNAN, NETTIE BURKE,
  MARY ELIZABETH DAVIS, JANET A. DUSTIN,
  ROSAMUND GARNER, VICTORIA D. GARRETT,
  JANE R. HALPIN, NANCY A. HARVEY, JOAN HURST,
  ARTEMIS S. LAMPATHAKIS, KATHERINE R. LEITCH,
  VIRGINIA W. McCOY, MARY EVELYN McKINNEY,
  CLEO E. PETROFF, TAMMY PRESLEY, SHERYL A.
  PROHOVICH, KATHLEEN T. SHEA, *Staff Assistants*
M. KATHLEEN HOGAN, *Indexer*

Foreword

A pleasant discovery we made in the course of planning this book was that a remarkable array of hidden corners can still be found in one of the most developed nations on earth. Actually, we found such an abundance of places off the beaten path that we faced a difficult task in deciding which to include. Almost every person involved in the project knew of several remote niches that he or she considered ideal subjects. Unfortunately we could not include all the many places that were suggested. Instead we decided to concentrate on secluded spots within seven distinct regions: the Great Basin, the Chesapeake Bay, the northern prairie, Michigan's Upper Peninsula, the Gulf Coast, the Ozarks, and the Four Corners area.

We chose to explore these seven regions because of the great geographic and cultural diversity they offer, and because each possesses a discernible character perhaps best seen in the wilderness areas, small towns, and rural byways that are America's hidden corners. During a year's time, our writers and photographers traveled to numerous out-of-the-way locales within these regions. Writer Chris Lee and photographer Annie Griffiths visited the West's vast Great Basin, an area of daunting deserts and range upon range of rumpled mountains. Leslie Allen and Nathan Benn traveled to the Chesapeake Bay, home to hardworking watermen who still follow the ways of their forebears.

In the sweeping prairies and badlands of the upper Midwest, writer Suzanne Venino and photographer Jim Brandenburg encountered a realm settled by a "steadfast people who survived the hard times when others packed up and left." Mary Ann Harrell and Lowell Georgia visited the beautiful Upper Peninsula—the arm of land edged by Lakes Superior, Michigan, and Huron—where they found a character "worthy of an independent planet."

The Gulf Coast's broad beaches, tangled mangrove islands, and labyrinthine delta lands drew writer Gene Stuart and photographer Dan Dry on a trip of some 1,500 miles. Tom O'Neill and Matt Bradley journeyed to the forested hills and hollows of the Ozarks, a region where "time-honored customs and folkways continue to be observed." And in the mountains, mesas, deserts, and canyons of the Four Corners area, Bob Morrison and Paul Chesley found a colossal landscape in which "the only things to rival the marvels of today are those awaiting discovery tomorrow."

In each of the places our writers and photographers visited, they found one common thread—a fierce independence on the part of those hardy souls who choose to live and work in places apart from the crowd. This book celebrates that spirit of independence as it takes you to some of the most picturesque of America's hidden corners.

PAUL D. MARTIN, *Managing Editor*

Wispy plume of Bridal Veil Falls spills down a sheer rock face just east of Telluride, Colorado. The falls once powered the clifftop generating station, which lit nearby gold and silver mines in the early 1900s.

6

`In the Shadow

of the Arrow'
The Great Basin

By CHRISTINE ECKSTROM LEE

Photographs by ANNIE GRIFFITHS

Artistry of the ancients, petroglyphs etched perhaps 2,000 years ago emblazon a boulder at the Grimes Point Archaeological Area near Fallon, Nevada. In the distance, the town's lights shine where the waters of a prehistoric lake once lapped; early hunters may have crouched behind boulders here to ambush game at the water's edge. Scholars still search for clues to the little-known lifeway of the first peoples of the Great Basin, a vast region of the West that remains largely untouched.

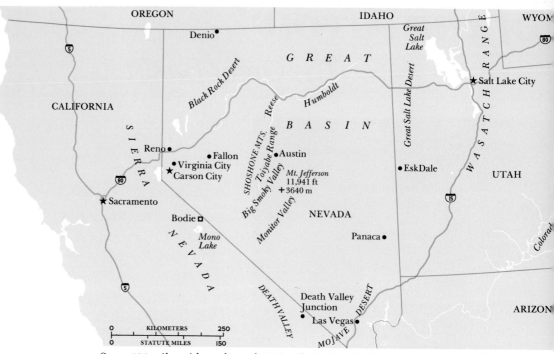

Some 600 miles wide and nearly 900 miles in length, the Great Basin spreads over most of Nevada and portions of surrounding states. Here desert valleys ribbed with towering mountain ranges shape a starkly dramatic landscape.

If Indian voices ever sang of a great white mountain where the ancestors lived, the song is lost, gone to the place where unremembered songs echo. The Indians were Shoshone, and along with the Paiute, Mono, and Washo, they once roamed the vast region of the West known as the Great Basin. Stretching across more than 200,000 square miles between the California Sierra and the Wasatch of Utah, north toward the Columbia River and south past Death Valley, the Great Basin—desert-dry in its sun-cracked valleys and pin-striped with snowy peaks—was so named because its waters have no outlet to the sea. Viewed by early travelers, traders, and settlers as supremely uninhabitable, the Great Basin was the last region of the United States outside Alaska to be penetrated and explored. An area where population—both ancient and modern—is measured not in people per square mile but in square miles per person, the Great Basin remains unknown, a land full of secrets.

The Indians of the Great Basin were scorned by early explorers as backward and wretched for choosing to live in so terrible a place. More recently their lifeway has been admired for its spare sophistication and keen timing to the clockwork of an unforgiving land. Survival was an art demanding absolute perfection. Some Indians of the Basin were said to describe their life with the saying, "In the shadow of the arrow."

Great Basin Indian culture has left little for the archaeologist to ponder. From scattered bits of lore and simple artifacts, scholars pieced together a tentative picture of a people living on the Basin's lower slopes and in its valleys, uncluttered hunter-gatherers forever chasing the seasons. Nothing suggested that this was not true.

Then in 1977, a Forest Service biologist surveying the highest peak in central Nevada, 11,941-foot Mount Jefferson, noticed some rocks just below the summit, unnaturally arranged in a ring. News of the sighting reached Dr. David Hurst Thomas of the American Museum of Natural History, an archaeologist who has worked at prehistoric sites in central Nevada since the 1960s. He climbed Mount Jefferson with a field crew in 1978 and found near the summit the remains of an entire Shoshone village, littered with thousands of artifacts—arrowheads, spear points, pottery sherds, pipes, beads, and tools. He called the village Alta Toquima after the range in which Mount Jefferson lies; it is among the highest Indian settlements ever found in North America, and its discovery opens new channels of thought about the lives of the first Americans. But what is more remarkable is that Alta Toquima was undisturbed, apparently unseen and untouched since the day centuries ago when the last Shoshone left, never to return.

A continent's worth of clouds seemed to slide past slowly above our heads as we walked through the ghost village of Alta Toquima. Photographer Annie Griffiths and I had hiked to the summit of Mount Jefferson, led by archaeologist Brian Hatoff of the Bureau of Land Management office in Carson City. Brian had worked with Dr. Thomas on the excavation of Alta Toquima during the summer of 1981, and he knew the site well. From where we stood, at an elevation of some 11,000 feet, we were as high as we could be for hundreds of miles around. It was mid-October, and early snows blanketed huge swaths of the summit tableland—a mile-wide, boulder-strewn, treeless plateau with ground so rocky and brittle and cold it seemed to crackle as we walked or clink if we stubbed our boots in the soil. A mile below us, Big Smoky Valley spread featureless and pale, and above its flats the 11,000-foot ramparts of the Toiyabe Range rose in a flashy parade of peaks, iced white with snow. In all the land we surveyed there were far more mountains than people, and the faint road we could see across the valley looked as unimportant as a scratch on a bison's hide.

"A lot more Shoshones have walked in here than people like us," Brian said as we crouched inside a crude ring of rocks that was once the foundation of a "wickiup"—a tepee-like home roofed with timbers and pine boughs. The Shoshones wore clothes of animal skins and woven sagebrush, and they ambushed game such as the bighorn sheep and harvested pine nuts from the trees on the steep slope below the village. Water came from a nearby spring. In the glaring sun and thin dry air, the bubbling water was almost intoxicating, sweet and icy, and dearer than gold in the arid Great Basin.

"These people were ingenious," Brian said. "They not only moved with the seasons, but they exploited different environmental zones—vertically. While it was summer in the valley, up here it was fall, and they were harvesting pine nuts." Alta Toquima was occupied only in the summer. "Living up here was a revolutionary idea. The Shoshone had no domestic plants or livestock. And we can't reconstruct their psychology—we don't know much about their religion. But they are more complicated than first meets the eye. Like the Great Basin."

We camped that night near the spring.   *(Continued on page 18)*   11

Two-day climb of Nevada's Mount Jefferson begins with a warmth-giving hot springs breakfast in Monitor Valley for author Chris Lee and Bureau of Land Management archaeologist Brian Hatoff. On a plateau near the summit (below), Chris and Brian hike toward their destination—Alta Toquima, at 11,000 feet, one of the highest Indian villages in North America. Discovered in 1977, Alta Toquima provided a summer home to Shoshone families beginning around A.D. 1000.

At top, Chris and Brian examine a village house ring, once roofed with timbers and pine boughs.

PAGES 14-15: Steam rises from Dianas Punch Bowl, a hot spring crater in Monitor Valley.

In a rock climber's paradise he calls "Elephant Land," explorer Alvin McLane nimbly leaps across jumbled stone slabs on his way to the top of a 150-foot-high rock tower (right). He then rappels down the sheer face of the tower (left). McLane found the jagged formations of Elephant Land in a remote and seldom-seen corner of northwest Nevada.

Sucking winds swept the summit, and I imagined that bison surrounded my tent, huffing hot air, stamping the frost. Although we were in the tundra zone, exposed to the vagaries of the sky, Brian, Annie, and I all remarked in the morning that we had been warmer at Alta Toquima than during the two previous nights of camping at lower, more sheltered places. "The Indians probably knew that, too," said Brian. "Discovering these things is what's so much fun about working in the Basin. It's not improbable that there are more Alta Toquimas to be found. We've really just begun to look."

Exploring the Great Basin and just "having a look" is more than an occupation for Alvin McLane; it's his hobby, sport, and favorite pleasure. Alvin currently works for a mining company as a field foreman, but in his 25 years in Nevada his jobs have ranged from blue collar to white collar to goose-down collar. "Most of my life I've been a free lance," Alvin said. "I've been a ripsawyer, a spelunker, map cataloger, writer, photographer, house painter, consulting hydrologist, historical researcher, archaeological surveyer, ski patroller, bibliographer, rock climber, mountaineer, and a high-altitude ant collector. When I first came here I worked at a trailer lot."

Alvin came to Reno from his native West Virginia. "My brother came west and said, 'Alvin, it's great, come on out.' So I got a big map of the U. S. and spread it on the floor, and the whole Great Basin was

Treasure at his fingertips, miner-gemologist Al Lombardo "stopes"—or removes—turquoise from the wall of his Nevada mine. At right, turquoise Lombardo has cut and polished gleams beside chunks of unprocessed stone.

empty, covered with stippled dots showing desert. And I thought, 'I wonder what's there?' It's irresistible! How can you not go out and see what fills a big blank space on the map? That's what I've been doing ever since, finding out what's out there."

Alvin's curiosity is matched by his protective feelings about special places and things he has discovered during his trips into the Basin backcountry. On one of the few spaces on the walls in Alvin's home not lined with books is a photograph of a bristlecone pine—the gnarled western tree that can live for millennia. Alvin believes he has found the largest living bristlecone pine. "It's 40 feet in circumference," he said.

Alvin delights in the smaller discoveries as well. "Oh my goodness, the things I've found! I've found Indian petroglyphs and pictographs—at unrecorded sites—and I've found abandoned pioneer wagons out in the desert. There are places where you can still see the old wagon wheel ruts." To the question "Where?" Alvin always answers, "In the Great Basin."

"We don't have a Grand Canyon or a Yosemite, but I like all the hidden surprises I find that people don't know about," Alvin said. "It's ironic, but there are no national parks in the Great Basin, a region with a multitude of beautiful places. People have just overlooked this whole area. I can go to my secret places and not be trampled by a horde of people. No one is ever there."

Alvin probably would have preferred that we were blindfolded when he took Annie Griffiths and me to one of his favorite hidden corners, a place he calls "Elephant Land." It lies in northwest Nevada, near the fissured expanse of the Black Rock Desert. "I first came here in about 1961," Alvin said as we drove across a wafer-flat valley, kicking up a trail of dust, en route to Elephant Land. "I was checking an old topographic map and I saw this speckled area that said 'rocky,' so I decided to have a look. Here's the turn." In the middle of the mountain-ringed expanse of sage flats, with virtually no trace of humanity in sight, at the crossing of two barely perceptible dirt roads, a pink toilet marked the turn-off to Elephant Land. "Somebody out here has a little humor," said Alvin. "I guess we'll call this Commode Junction."

Alvin named Elephant Land after a rock shaped like an elephant's head, listed by that name in an old journal he was reading. "I wanted to honor the original name," he explained. Alvin has also attached names to about 30 of Nevada's estimated 300 mountain ranges. "That's the kind of country this is. They don't even have names for some of the features out here."

In the distance, among the brown, bare-ribbed hills, stood one with a sawtoothed crown: Elephant Land. We drove toward the peak up a wash, or draw—a dry gully like those that furrow mountains throughout the Basin. When we reached the crest of the hill, we found ourselves in the middle of Elephant Land, a fantasy world of huge, wildly shaped rock formations, a playground scaled for gamboling behemoths. For several hours we romped with Alvin in Elephant Land, scrambling atop 50-foot-high boulders, shinnying up stone columns and pinnacles, and peering across the dizzying distances of the Basin through the window rocks of Alvin's geological jungle gym.

Near the end of the day, I paused to watch as Alvin, muscular and sturdy as a French voyageur, scampered up a 150-foot rock tower with his climbing ropes, and rappelled down the sheer face, springing from the rock in a slinky-toy descent, pedaling his legs in the air, yipping and hooting like a coyote, deliriously joyful. We headed back to Reno at dusk. Errant beach balls of tumbleweed bounced, stalled, and danced crazily into the road. Sunset reddened the empty hills, its last line of light creeping higher up the slopes until darkness came.

"Some of my most memorable experiences out here," said Alvin, "have been sitting alone under a piñon pine when the night is so crisp, thinking about how infinitesimal I am compared to the world around me—the mountains, the land here, the whole earth—and just to look up at the stars and think of how many other universes there are, and universes within universes." Clouds raced in the night sky. "Out here we have the freedom to roam. Some of this land is so beautiful it seems a sacrilege to enter. It's the way the pioneers saw it, it's the way the Indians left it, the way God made it. It makes you feel free."

The freedom Alvin prizes was just one of many dreams that led to the gradual exploration and lightly peppered settlement of the Great Basin. The possibility of what lay within the Basin's unknown territory fueled imaginations—and myths as strange and fantastic as the lands they glorified. Among the New World Spaniards of the 16th century, the rumor that the rich and fabled Seven Cities of Cíbola were somewhere north of Mexico gave way to the Legend of Sierra Azul—a blue mountain of silver—located near the Basin's southern boundary. Sierra Azul even appears on maps as late as 1852.

Some maps of the late 18th century showed a "Sea of the West" reaching across the Basin to the Rockies, and the story of the mythical San Buenventura River—first envisioned as a waterway to the Orient and later as a passage to the Pacific—persisted until the mid-19th century when explorer John C. Frémont dispelled the river's existence with an ironic touch: It was he who named the Basin, realizing that its waters never reach the sea. The quest for truth in the tales lured many expeditions just past the edges of the Basin, but not until the 19th century did white men begin to cross its rugged interior reaches. The first were trappers in search of fur, followed in the 1840s by the consecutive tides of emigrants and forty-niners rushing to California. The Basin was an ordeal to survive, not a place to live.

The first emigrants to choose the Basin as a home were the Mormons, seeking a new land where they could practice their faith undisturbed. They settled in the Salt Lake Valley in 1847 and steadily established towns southward along the eastern edge of the Basin, hoping eventually to reach the sea and set up trade routes for a huge kingdom they planned to found in the west, to be known as Deseret. Their dream of an independent desert nation spanning the Basin did not materialize, but they succeeded in planting communities around the region and in farming a land generally viewed as untillable.

In the mid-1800s, the discovery of gold and silver in the bleak hills of the Basin dramatically altered the region's history and development. Following the silver strike at the Comstock Lode in 1859, and the subsequent birth of rollicking Virginia City, fortune seekers began to comb the mountains of the Basin, panning streams, chipping at rocks, digging holes in hillsides, and staking claims. Boomtowns were assembled and dismantled overnight like stage sets, and the Basin was enlivened with traveling shows of entire cities, moving from place to place to play the next big strike.

Sweet scent of sage and the bleats of sheep fill the air as a herder tends his flock near the Nevada-Oregon border. Since the late 19th century, sheep and cattle ranches have thrived in many of the Great Basin's northern valleys.

Praising the Lord with music, children of the Order of Aaron, a Christian community in EskDale, Utah, rehearse for a concert. Nearly half of the order's 85 members play in the orchestra, which tours the state. The late Maurice L. Glendenning organized the remote desert community in 1955. Its motto, "Education Unlimited," expresses one of the order's chief concerns. At EskDale's Montessori school, Rietta Hartlauer assists Natalie Anderson with her lessons (right). The community works toward economic self-sufficiency; after helping to empty a truckload of potatoes, Fay Carlson pedals home (right, lower). Beginning with the Mormon settlement of Salt Lake Valley in 1847, the Basin's isolated regions have attracted groups seeking to practice their beliefs in peace and solitude.

Mining still shapes the Basin. Much of it is done by big corporations tapping reserves of copper, tungsten, lead, and iron, as well as various nonmetallic minerals, or by companies retrieving invisible particles of gold using sophisticated and costly new technology. But the days of the independent solitary prospector have not completely passed. The man who roams the hills for a find, following his instinct or a tip from an old Indian, equipped with a pick, pan, and shovel—and unwavering faith—is more than a legend of the American West: He is still here, searching for the mother lode.

Al Lombardo was running short of luck. A native New Yorker, he was laid off his job as a mechanical engineer in Florida. At that point he decided to become a nomad, and he headed west to treasure hunt. He prospected in Death Valley and then turned north for Alaska to search for gold, traveling from Fairbanks to the Arctic Circle. The first thing Al found was an old five-dollar bill from the gold rush days, which he sold for seven dollars. Gold was low, gas was high, and his funds ran out. On Al's way back to Florida, his truck broke down smack in the middle of the Great Basin, and he had no money to repair it. "I was sitting here in Austin, Nevada, with 17 cents in my pocket, having a cup of coffee in the International Hotel," said Al. "I was desperate, and when you're desperate sometimes you pull rabbits out of hats."

Al went to work in a turquoise mine north of Austin. "Then I started to like the area," he explained. "I liked the openness. Wow! Hundreds of miles of public land and who does it belong to? You! That's what the 1872 Mining Law is all about. If you find a mineral, you can develop it. It's yours. The Great Basin is one of the last places you can do this." He learned about turquoise and went prospecting. He bought a $1,500 interest in an undeveloped claim held by an old Indian in Austin. "I just had a gut feeling about this deposit," Al said. "I didn't know why, but I knew it was valuable." He bought the whole claim, started to mine, and struck a lode of precious turquoise that is now probably worth a fortune.

I met Al inside the turquoise-colored metal building on the edge of Austin that serves as the mine office, display room, store, lab, and manufacturing facility for the Lombardo Turquoise Milling & Mining Company, Inc. "The Great Basin's a place that sounds like Siberia to people who haven't been here," said Al, as we hopped into his truck to head for the rough hills northwest of town—and Al's mine. "What's so unreal," said Al, "is that the gemstone wealth of the United States is untapped. And it's right here. This area has been mined for gold, silver, and strategic metals. That's it. Gems are just sitting out there in the hills; you just have to go out and find them."

We turned onto a rutted dirt road and began winding up into the mountains. A dusting of snow revealed the texture of the land like a powdered fingerprint. We climbed higher, stopping near a spring to put chains on the tires and slip into four-wheel drive. "Wait till you see where my mine is," said Al. "The eagles fly by with oxygen masks. It's

Like Gothic spires, pinnacled formations in Cathedral Gorge State Park soar above the rolling desert near Panaca, in eastern Nevada. Erosion of the gorge's soft bentonite clay has created a fantasy world of such natural sculptures.

one of the most beautiful primitive areas in the state. It looks prehistoric." We saw eagles and mountain bluebirds as we edged along a precipitous slope to the crest of a ridge. Down a short, nearly vertical hill was the mine entrance, a door leading into the mountain.

Al calls his workings the Shoshone Mine. "I've heard an Indian legend that says the great god took the water from the lake that used to fill the valley below. He placed it up on this mountain, parted the clouds, and made the water into turquoise." We entered Al's tunnel wearing miner's hard hats with lamps, carrying picks, chisels, and a screwdriver. "Everyone thinks mining is so romantic," said Al. "It's the hardest, dirtiest, rottenest job in the whole world. And dangerous—you could blow yourself up. But it's worth every bit of it. Three weeks ago we blasted and $10,000 worth of turquoise blew up all over the place. I didn't even know it was there. It was a blind vein. Thousands of dollars of stone just fell into my hands. It's like finding a treasure."

We walked to the end of the tunnel, to work the blind vein Al had struck. I shone my light on the back wall where narrow streamers of turquoise streaked the dark rock like dazzling bolts of blue lightning. "This turquoise is flawless, the highest quality," Al said, "and in beauty it rivals the turquoise of the ancient mines of Persia and the Sinai."

Al showed me how to "stope" the vein—using a pick and a chisel to work the turquoise out of the rock. Tiny sparks flashed as I struck the wall near a vein with a pick; with a chisel or a screwdriver, I loosened the turquoise and scratched it out with my fingernails, slowly filling one hand with puzzle-piece-size chips. "You're holding hundreds of dollars there," said Al. "I can take out my product in my pocket," he explained. "The object of mining is not to tear a mountain down; it's greenbacks. Fifty years from now, you would hardly know I'd been here. This is a complete hand operation, like the way the old-timers worked." A small train track leads from the back of the tunnel outside to the mountain's edge, and a hundred-year-old ore car carries mined rock along the track to the cliff. The debris is dumped from a wooden trestle Al built, copying its design from old photographs.

With a small bucket of turquoise, we stepped into the cold sunshine outside the mine. "The people who live in the Great Basin, making it work, are people who have survived," said Al. "I feel like a modern-day settler, because this frontier is still alive. Ten years ago I would never have thought that I would be up here, drilling a hole into a mountain. If I were to sell this mine, I'd sell feelings I can't get anywhere else, a natural high, the mystery of the search. What's beyond the next foot in this mine? Is it the Blue Room—the Comstock of turquoise? Who would trade that?"

I was haunted by a sense of discovery and of wanting to search wherever I traveled in the Basin. The empty hills are charged with tension, electric with secrecy. Driving up the Reese River Valley as a storm approached, I saw vistas that seemed like images of the day the earth was born. Black clouds rushed low across the mountains, breaking open to let the sun illuminate the white peaks, then closing, swirling, and opening again, as if the earth were preparing to reveal its masterwork to the heavens. Thick cotton clouds filled the canyons between the peaks, like steam rising from a landscape still hot from creation.

The Reese River traces a thin course up the valley toward its meeting with the waters of the Humboldt. The scant water that flows from the mountains of the Basin or percolates through the earth in small crystal springs seems wept from the arid wastes, the tears of stones.

Cattle scatter across northern Nevada, spaced wide in proportion to the huge amounts of grazing land each needs, and large ranches fill many of the Basin's valleys. In the wake of the 19th-century miners, cattlemen and sheepmen moved into the Basin, and their ranching operations are a major industry of the region today. Sometimes the Great Basin seems like an empty stage, and when the play begins it looks as if most of the characters are cows.

Up north near the Oregon border, I visited a ranch where most of the players were sheep. The Dufurrena family manages the ranch, and like many of the area's sheepmen, Buster Dufurrena's ancestors were Basques, the people whose homeland lies in the Pyrénées mountains of France and Spain. Although fewer Basques come to America each year, and despite the decline in the number of big sheep ranches, the Basque herders and their descendants remain at the heart of the Basin sheep industry, as they have for nearly a century.

Buster's young son, Hank, and his bride of one year, Ginny, live and work on the ranch and plan to continue the family sheep and cattle business. Before dawn one fall morning, Annie Griffiths and I drove into the hills with Hank and Ginny to check the flock and count sheep.

"Nowadays, it's hard to make a ranch work," said Hank. "We have about 2,300 sheep and 350 head of cattle right now, and we have to run the sheep about 70 miles north to south through the year. This land is pretty rough. You have to keep moving all the time."

We bounced over the top of a sage-studded hill and eased down to the clearing where the ranch's two herders, Juan and Miguel, were camped in a canvas tent. Sunlight leaked in along the horizon, and I saw the herd huddled along a sheltered flank of the mountain, grayish like a patch of old snow. Juan, Miguel, and Hank bounded up the slope with surefooted strides, and we followed behind. For more than an hour, we helped Hank check and count the flock, funneling past him in single file the leaping, bleating lines of sheep—their hoofs drumming and tin bells clanging in the sound-amplifying desert air.

Hank talked about life on the ranch as we picked a path back down the hill. "We all used to rodeo," he said. "I used to calf rope, bulldog, team ride—we all grew up with a rope in our hands. It's a part of living here. Working on a ranch gives you a good feeling, like you've really accomplished something, every day."

Ginny, her cheeks bright pink like a doll's in the morning chill, talked about their wedding. "I made my own wedding dress," she said, "in between shoveling manure! The chores have to get done. On our wedding day I rode up the mountain in a truck with the bridesmaids, with curlers in my hair. We got stuck once and had to get out and push, but we got there. We had the ceremony in a meadow in the mountains. It was so pretty. And the whole community threw a reception for us. For a while I thought living on a ranch was too hard. I remember once I was ready to give it up, and all of a sudden something snapped and I got the confidence. To me, this is heaven."

Far down in the southern reaches of the Great Basin, a few miles from one of the most fearsome landscapes in North America—the place called Death Valley—stands a small, former borax mining town known as Death Valley Junction. The California town was about to crumble into the sunbaked earth from which its adobe buildings had come when Tom Williams and Marta Becket limped into town with a flat tire. It was Good Friday 1967 and Tom and Marta were returning home to New York. Marta is a dancer, and Tom, her husband, the impresario. Together they traveled over the country presenting Marta's one-woman show of ballet and dance-pantomime. When they broke down in Death Valley Junction, Marta wandered down the street and spotted an old theater—and imagined it as a wonderful studio.

"We thought it over carefully," said Tom, "and about an hour later decided to move here. We found the town manager, who reluctantly agreed to rent us the building for $45 a month. We gave him a dollar deposit and a handshake, and somehow we've been here ever since."

Death Valley Junction is on the way to nowhere, some 75 miles from Las Vegas. It lies in the middle of scrub desert where the silence is so complete that the scratchy scamperings of lizards in the sand or the rushing beat of a bird's wings above seem clear and distinct, and where you can hear the texture of the wind. Distant ranges of gaunt mountains frame the town, a long colonnaded complex of white-washed adobe buildings with several empty adobe homes behind.

The theater stands at the end of the main complex. Tom and Marta decided to fix it up so Marta could present her shows there. They named it the Amargosa Opera House, after a nearby river. Fame did not come quickly for Tom and Marta, but after 15 years of performances—occasionally to the applause of a single guest—the opera house now attracts audiences that seem to attend in defiance of the town's isolation. "I really have a wonderful feeling for this place," Marta said. "It's like time has stopped. In New York you have a constant reminder of time going faster than you can. And you can't catch up with it. Here it's stopped. I can catch up with time." We walked outside in the warm sunshine. "This is a fairy tale," said Marta. "I knew what I wanted to do, what I had to do. So I kept searching for a place. Anything worthwhile in life is a luxury. My luxury is my life here in this little desert town, where I can pursue my art as my heart tells me."

A few years ago, Tom and Marta bought the town of Death Valley Junction to preserve it. It has been listed in the National Register of Historic Places, and the couple has begun to restore the other buildings. A small hotel and a Mexican restaurant have opened in the complex. Tom and Marta hope one day to create a desert campus for field study groups from all over the West.

Marta looked at the whitewashed buildings. "I owe something to this town," she said. "I can't imagine anywhere else in the world where I could have done this." I think Marta spoke for many of the people who make their lives in the far reaches of the Great Basin when she said, "Out here I have an empty canvas where I can paint my dreams."

Dancer in the desert, Marta Becket performs before an audience she painted inside the Amargosa Opera House in Death Valley Junction, California. Her shows have brought admiring patrons—and new life—to the former ghost town.

Images from a bygone era linger in Bodie, California, a ghost town on the eastern slope of the Sierra Nevada. The town boomed after the discovery of gold nearby in 1859, once boasting a population of 10,000—and the wickedest reputation in the West. Its remains, now preserved as the Bodie State Historic Park, include a teacher's desk (left), a detail from the barber shop (above), a place setting in the home of a former madam (below, left), and a roulette wheel from one of the town's many casinos.

FOLLOWING PAGES: Winter snows shroud Bodie, a monument to the lost dreams of another time.

They

Follow the Water

The Chesapeake Bay

By LESLIE ALLEN

Photographs by NATHAN BENN

Bounty of the Bay: Centuries-old technique of pound-netting yields a plentiful catch for watermen of Tangier Island, Virginia. Nets strung from stakes driven into the bottom of the Bay guide the fish—spot, flounder, trout, and menhaden—into a large trap. Little changed by time, many such tested fishing methods still prevail among the hardworking seafood harvesters of the Chesapeake.

*F*ollow the water. It was a refrain I heard repeatedly along the Chesapeake Bay and its many tributaries. "I follow the water," said an old man in Ewell, Maryland, "just like my daddy. And his daddy before him." He was referring to lives spent harvesting seafood in small boats, to vicissitudes of weather and catches and markets, to good years and lean ones. "My boy, he follows the water, too." Generations succeed each other in the water trades as surely as yielding seasons; it has been that way for more than a century.

Until recently, change came slowly to the Chesapeake. Often it came, and still does, in the gestures, sweeping or subtle, of nature. Ten thousand years ago—a wink in geological time—the Bay as we know it today did not exist. Glacial melt was still raising the Atlantic, backing up the Susquehanna River and flooding the ancient valley that would become the Chesapeake. Slowly the water spread to its present dimensions: nearly 200 miles long, with an average width of 15 miles, an average depth of 21 feet, and some 8,000 miles of rumpled tidal shoreline shared by what are now Maryland and Virginia. The Chesapeake was to become one of the nation's largest bays. And, thanks to life-endowing torrents from the nearly 50 rivers that feed it, it also became one of the continent's richest estuaries—a seafood cornucopia with annual catches now valued at more than a hundred million dollars.

The Chesapeake's chief explorer, Captain John Smith, was moved to eloquence on the subject of Bay country when, in 1612, he wrote: "Heaven and earth never agreed better to frame a place for man's habitation." Others at the time shared his assessment. Smith's "fruitful and delightsome land" nurtured the New World's first English settlements. By the mid-1600s, great tobacco plantations dotted points of land around the Bay, many taking hold along the deepwater rivers of the Chesapeake's western shore. In the 1800s, tiny farming and fishing villages shared the gentle vistas. Those who wrested a living from the Bay came to be called watermen; their culture spread to every cove and creek, yet their small communities remained remarkably insular.

Not until 1952 did a bridge link the Bay's Eastern Shore, a narrow peninsula between the Chesapeake and the Atlantic, to its western shore. Now, the entire region lies within a day's drive for millions of Americans. Throughout the year mid-Atlantic residents come to sail, swim, or fish, to hunt or simply to soak up the calm of the Bay's marshlands. Less happily, the Bay is also the recipient of refuse from its 64,000-square-mile watershed—agricultural runoff, sewage, and industrial wastes that alter its delicate ecological balance. "This old Bay's under pressure," say local watermen, who with a shake of their heads will also tell you their catches just aren't what they used to be.

Despite these and other environmental problems, life on the Bay still moves to the quiet beat of nature's rhythms. Above all, the seasonal cycle brings variety to this watery web. In towns barely touched by time—places such as Chance, Mobjack, Birdsnest, or Bivalve—spring and summer always bring crabbing, fall and winter oystering. "In between" may bring fishing or eeling, hunting or boat painting, or just hanging around the general store spinning yarns that improve with each telling. In these parts, the view from the road is, in a sense, of the backyard. The front yard is the water itself.

Most isolated of all Chesapeake communities are Tangier Island,

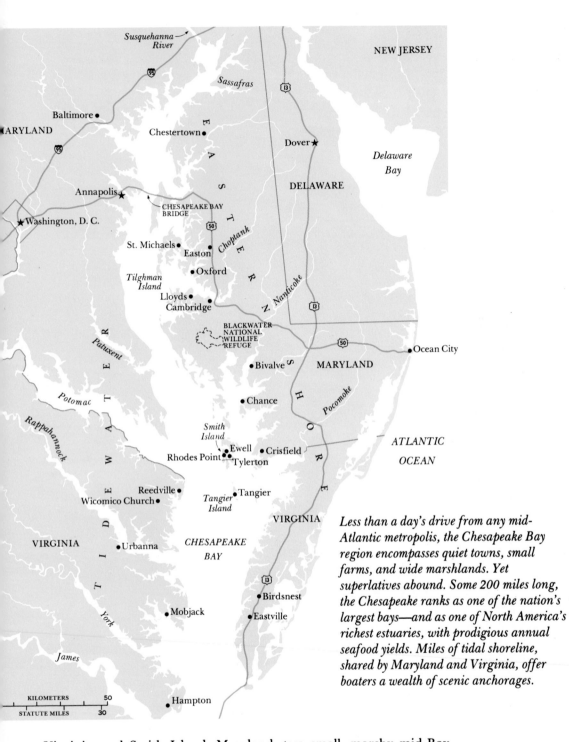

Less than a day's drive from any mid-Atlantic metropolis, the Chesapeake Bay region encompasses quiet towns, small farms, and wide marshlands. Yet superlatives abound. Some 200 miles long, the Chesapeake ranks as one of the nation's largest bays—and as one of North America's richest estuaries, with prodigious annual seafood yields. Miles of tidal shoreline, shared by Maryland and Virginia, offer boaters a wealth of scenic anchorages.

Virginia, and Smith Island, Maryland, two small, marshy mid-Bay spots across the state line from each other. Both were settled before 1700; since then, newcomers have been so scarce that only a very few surnames—but countless nicknames—exist. Among Tangier's 900 people, Crocketts, Parkses, and Pruitts predominate, as does the Cornish accent of their forebears. On Smith, the names Evans, Tyler, Bradshaw, and Marshall include most of (Continued on page 42)

Flanked by an honor guard, marchers proudly bearing U. S. and state flags open the Crab Derby parade in Crisfield, Maryland, a town where the tasty crustacean rules in commerce and in legend. Below, high school musicians enjoy themselves just before the parade. Featured at the annual salute: a crab race, with contestants representing nearly every state; a "Miss Crustacean" competition; and mounds of crab cakes and other Bay specialties. During the three-day event, politicians and day-tripping tourists mingle with local watermen.

Homes and outbuildings crowd together on scarce solid ground along the waterfront of Tylerton, Maryland. Like other Smith Islanders, Tylertonians earn renown for their cultivation of soft-shell, or molted, crabs, a Chesapeake delicacy. At left, Dallas Bradshaw selects "peelers"—crabs about to molt—from his dockside saltwater holding pens. Packed with ice and seaweed after molting, soft-shell "whales," the largest variety, await transport to market (right).

LOWELL GEORGIA

the population of 550. In the case of either island, getting there is half the fun. The mainland link to both Smith and Tangier is the daily mail boat from Crisfield, a jaunty town on Maryland's Eastern Shore. Down at the County Dock, where I waited for the 12:30 boat to Tangier, I found myself at Crisfield's social hub. Local people came and went while crab boat captains idled at the pier. Retired watermen—hands folded atop their walking sticks, baseball caps pulled low—perched on the "liar's bench" and offered sporadic commentary on the intensive preparations under way. Aboard the mail boat, mail is but one cargo: Groceries, suitcases, kitchen appliances, baskets of crabs, and 25 passengers all found a place on the *Dorolena* for the hour-and-a-half trip.

On Tangier, even at the height of daily comings-and-goings, there is a calm that suggests an old Dutch landscape painting. Light plays on the island's sky-blue harbor and its tawny marshes, on its white workboats and equally white frame buildings. All in a line along the three narrow ridges, Tangier's only high ground, windows of well-proportioned homes glow brightly as the sun goes down. The island's people are similarly handsome: tall, strong, fair-haired, and even-featured. The absence of worldly diversions suits most just fine. "What goes on in the outside world is not material," said Ray Crockett, who runs the Double Six confectionary. "We don't study by it."

On Tangier and Smith, following the water is virtually the only way to make a living. Islanders handle their boats with superb precision, and both craft and owners are recognized even at great distances. Early one morning, I went out crabbing with Mike "Psychey Mikey" Thorne, a hardworking young Tangierman. The horizon enclosed several examples of classic, sharp-bowed Chesapeake workboats similar to Mike's 45-foot craft. Suddenly Mike dropped a wire-mesh crab pot on deck and pointed at a speck in the distance. "There's a Marylander, working in Virginia waters," he said, noting casually that this was illegal. "How can you tell where it's from?" I inquired. He surely thought my question silly. "If a new car showed up on your block," he replied, "you'd know it too, wouldn't you?"

Island life focuses on the church almost as much as it does on the water. Methodism took hold during the War of 1812, when preacher Joshua Thomas warned British troops encamped on Tangier that their planned attack on Baltimore would fail—and so became known as a prophet. As "Parson of the Islands," he sailed up and down the Chesapeake in the *Methodist,* spreading the gospel from one town to the next. Throughout the region, Thomas's legacy still holds strong.

On Smith Island, bumper stickers and pier post signs proclaim: "Jesus on the Island." Summertime brings well-known evangelists to Smith's large outdoor revivals; the first, in 1889, was held under a tent fashioned, with island ingenuity, from a schooner mainsail. More than the island's spiritual center, the church is the governing body for Smith Island. There is no local government of any other kind.

A special kind of group support, in the form of the "testimony meeting," also binds islanders. One Sunday, before regular church services began, I attended the testimony meeting at the church in Ewell, Smith's largest town. Indian summer's mellow warmth poured in as church members rose in turn to speak. A lay leader moved quietly among them, facing each speaker squarely, smiling and nodding encouragement. Accounts of workaday trials mingled with the plain-spoken litany of thanksgiving. One man, his face deeply furrowed, spoke of a recent storm that had roiled the Bay with gale-force winds.

"We thought of all those crab pots out there," he said, "and we thought for sure we'd lose them all." But, he continued, no pots were lost and the price of crabs doubled. "I want to thank the Lord for everything—for oysters, crabs, and everything else." His voice sank to a

Faithful to Smith Island's Methodist past, Charles Marsh leads a testimony meeting in Tylerton; in Ewell, a summer revival holds two congregants rapt.

FOLLOWING PAGES: Built at the century's turn, the skipjack Sigsbee, *one of the last of such sailing workboats, drags an oyster dredge along the soft Bay bottom.*

slow, gravelly whisper. When he finished, others gathered round to offer a handshake and a few words.

Though its three towns all boast their own sparkling church, Smith has only one minister to go around. Every Sunday, he does just that: from Ewell to Rhodes Point by car; from there by boat to Tylerton, separated from the main island by a narrow channel. But Smith has no doctors, and no high school. A medical emergency means a wait for a helicopter from the mainland. Education may mean a daily commute by "school boat" to Crisfield.

Tylerton has no cars. Of a Sunday, when workboats remain at their moorings, the loudest sounds are the strains of the splendid church choir, or perhaps the call of geese overhead. An island's island, Tylerton is a jewel in the Bay. On neat lawns, flowers bloom luxuriantly well into the fall. Mazelike on the water stretch rows of piers and crab shanties where, in summer, entire families work round the clock to harvest soft-shell, or molted, crabs favored by seafood connoisseurs.

In winter, ice calls long halts to all off-island movement. Then, eating well is the best revenge. Island women, Tylertonians especially, are fine cooks. Priscilla Bradshaw's Sunday dinner was enough to quicken a gourmet's pulse. The feast included crab imperial, oyster fritters, and broiled sea trout accompanied by potato salad, homemade rolls, pickled beets, and corn pudding. After dessert, apple custard pie, family and friends groaned and attempted to stand; but then Priscilla rushed in with a chocolate layer cake. *(Continued on page 48)*

Shadowy fingers of land enfold Cockrell Creek at sunset. Winding and branching, rivers that include the Rappahannock, York, James, and Potomac give the Chesapeake's western shore its labyrinthine contours. At left, the rising sun finds work under way aboard a typical "box stern." One waterman hauls rake-like tongs up from Bay-floor oyster beds while another sorts the muddy contents.

Hospitality goes out to everyone—with the possible exception of game wardens, or anyone else who "interferes" with hunting. "Here's the thing: We've got no industry and no farming. What comes here is the only thing we have to make a living from. And that means crabs, oysters, geese, and ducks. There's the difference between the sportsman and the working man." The speaker was 68-year-old Paul Marshall of Tylerton, and the crackling topic was the laws that had, during his lifetime, limited waterfowl hunting.

As young men, Paul and his brother Edward, 72, were known as Smith Island's best hunters. They engaged in the now outlawed form of hunting called market gunning—using enormous guns to shoot large numbers of birds for sale. I had seen one of Paul's old "punt guns" in Tylerton's little museum. It was 10 feet long and weighed 113 pounds. To use a punt gun, the hunter had to mount it in a boat, lie down alongside it, and at the moment he fired, lean away to avoid injury. One good shot into a bobbing flock might yield 20 birds.

"They used to shoot them for the fancy hotels and restaurants in Baltimore," Paul said. "First they'd bring them back to Tylerton to pick. There was a time when every bed on this island was a featherbed. And it took about 800 ducks to make one featherbed and two pillows."

By trade, Paul Marshall was a crab packer, but his mind never strayed far from waterfowl. In middle age, he took up the carving of decorative wooden decoys—a popular and increasingly lucrative local pastime—and gained repute as Smith Island's best carver. Orders for decoys came from as far as New England.

Out back, Paul's workshop is a two-room structure that has also served, at different times, as post office, grocery store, Red Cross sewing room, and the Marshall's first home. Whole wooden flocks perched on shelves and on tabletops. Each decoy had been crafted with a delicacy that revealed a deep tenderness for wildlife. It was only the first of many times that I sensed a waterman's unspoken ambivalence toward hunting.

In addition to decoys, Paul's waterfront shop contained large numbers of porcelain doorknobs, old bottles, seashells, and fossils. Like Paul, many watermen are anything but ambivalent about collecting; their varied finds usually result from leisure-time marsh wanderings that also make them skilled naturalists.

Tylerton's most impressive collection belongs to Allan Smith, a waterman with a soft voice and keen eyes. At his home, Allan showed me shoe box after shopping bag full of Indian artifacts: arrowheads by the hundred, pipes, axheads, scrapers, broken pottery. Mostly they represented the legacy of Bay area tribes that have all but vanished.

"This is just what I've collected in the last three years," Allan said. "I used to find these things when I was a boy and give them all away." He emptied the contents of one paper bag onto his kitchen table and sorted through it. He selected two arrowheads, each almost perfectly symmetrical, and offered them to me. "Now you take these," he insisted. "An old man once told me that nothing you give away is lost. It's kept in the memories of others."

As he put his collection away, Allan commented that centuries from now archaeologists would still be able to find Indian artifacts—that is, he added wryly, if the islands themselves are around. His remark reflected a grim fact: Large stretches of Bay shoreline, especially the edges of islands, are rapidly eroding. Maryland alone has lost some 25,000 acres over the past century. The causes are varied. The Bay is slowly being filled with river sediments that change its contours. Farming and development in its vast watershed speed this process. Then, too, land around the Bay sinks about an inch each decade. And all the while, wind and water continue their insatiable gnawing. A century ago, Sharp's Island held 400 acres; today Sharp's no longer exists. Among a dozen or more mid-Bay islands, only Smith and Tangier now hold communities. And almost everyone in both places can remember some little beach, some point of land that used to be.

In Crisfield, Lillian Todd remembers well a community that erosion destroyed—Holland Island, north of Smith. She was born in her grandmother's house there in 1894 and left in 1918, when the last inhabitants loaded their belongings on barges and moved away.

Lillian showed me faded photographs kept since girlhood: her home, herself, children sitting on a fence. "There were more than 300 people," she said. "We had a minister, a doctor, and two schoolteachers." Holland Island was a prosperous watermen's community. It was

Bivalves by the bushel bring hungry crowds to Urbanna, Virginia, for the town's autumn oyster festival. Here Wayne Judah tends a steaming batch, while busy shuckers open fresh oysters for customers who prefer theirs on the half shell.

largely self-sufficient, with vegetable gardens and, even in Lillian's time, herds of cattle and sheep. "I like for my mind to drift back there," she said. "We thought it was the garden spot of the Chesapeake Bay."

Throughout the region, villages have come and gone. In the Eastern Shore marshlands especially, many humps of hard land once held human life. A glance across that great wet prairie may take in such now abandoned, pine-covered hammocks. Though people are scarce, the

Camouflaged by swamp grass and cut cornstalks, Eastern Shore hunters lure geese into range with calls that mimic the birds' raucous honking. Decoys add to the artful deception. With migrating waterfowl in the thickest concentrations along the Atlantic flyway—more than half a million Canada geese, and ducks in the tens of thousands—the Chesapeake region offers exceptional hunting. From late fall through early winter, blinds in countless fields and marshy tumps become weekend lairs to local residents and urban sportsmen alike. Below, Canada geese take wing at Blackwater National Wildlife Refuge, an Eastern Shore haven for 240 species of birds.

marshes do claim hundreds of thousands of residents of another sort: wintering wildfowl, in the Atlantic flyway's largest numbers. All told, 240 species of birds spend at least part of each year here. They concentrate over the 14,263 acres of Blackwater National Wildlife Refuge, in Maryland's Dorchester County.

Every week, Guy Willey of Blackwater's staff surveys all the waterfowl using the refuge. It is an awesome task: As many as 25,000 Canada geese alone winter at Blackwater. But after 31 years at it, Guy can count a thousand birds faster than anyone else can count the fingers on two hands. One gray November morning, I climbed into a jeep and set out with Guy for a day of dizzying numbers. First stop was a large pond.

"You take these binoculars and see what you come up with," he said. The pond was a moving quilt of black, white, brown, and gray— Canadas. As I tried to count, long strings of geese, back from their morning feeding, glided in amid general honking; other birds took wing. "In the meantime," Guy said, "watch the ducks and see what species you've got. Those pintails and mallards are all spread out." I decided to give up on the geese and focus on the ducks. Guy spoke again:

Master of foxhounds Wilbur Ross Hubbard, 87, stands ready for the hunt. His collected horns, antique and modern, frame his portrait at age 30. Below, fox hunters ride to hounds near Hubbard's Chestertown, Maryland, home.

"Look at what just got up in the air! We've got to count them, too."

I quit. Like an artist with his paintbrush, Guy held a pen out at eye level, squinted, and quickly blocked off the scene before him. Fifteen hundred Canadas. Three hundred ducks, broken down by species.

"What we're looking for are trends," Guy said as we drove on. "I'm consistent—consistently right or consistently wrong—but whichever, it shows the trends. And I've definitely seen some changes since I've been here." The loss of ecologically sensitive aquatic grasses, waterfowl food, has caused a dramatic decline in ducks. "In the late '50s, I'd count 150,000 ducks. Now we only get about 25,000 a year."

In sky-darkening numbers, the Canadas still come down from the north. Throughout the region, they make a stirring sight as they pass overhead in near-perfect V-shaped formations, slender necks stretched southward. "Harvesting them is almost a necessity," Guy told me. "But the geese learn that Blackwater is a sanctuary, and they tend to feed within it. Those birds aren't as dumb as some hunters think."

In gusts of spray, we traveled by skiff through Blackwater's remote backland—a world of swamps, snaking rivers, hammocks, and sunken islands. Spiky cordgrasses rustled around and above us. Tall *Phragmites,* plumy grasses, bowed deeply in the wind. Set against this monochromatic wilderness, the displays of the birds were at their dazzling best. Two dozen whistling swans seemed a great snowflake drifting to earth. Guy pointed to a large nest in a distant clump of trees. I caught a brief glimpse of the two bald eagles that flew out of the nest before they disappeared. Guy had seen others that day; he thought there were 51 in the county. At Blackwater, the embattled bald eagle is making a precarious comeback.

As the bald eagle symbolizes the nation, so the Chesapeake has its own symbol in the skipjack. This graceful oyster boat is of more than local interest: It represents the country's last commercial sailing fleet. And like the bald eagle, the skipjack is an endangered species. At the turn of the century, hundreds raked their dredges over Bay oyster beds; fewer than three dozen remain. Maryland law, with few exceptions, allows dredging only from sailing vessels. Most watermen now harvest oysters from powerboats using long, scissor-like tongs.

"Why do I keep dredging?" Captain Wadie Murphy, owner of the 82-year-old skipjack *Sigsbee,* repeated my question. "It's all I've ever known. I love to sail and I love to catch oysters this way. I'd rather do this than anything else in the world."

It was 5 a.m. when we left Tilghman Island aboard *Sigsbee.* For the two-hour ride to the oyster bed, Wadie held the wheel while his crew of five escaped from the chill down below. As a crewman heated coffee, talk focused on the rumored locations of good oysters, then wandered aimlessly. The clinking of silverware punctuated bursts of CB static. Finally, the rising sun revealed, at the bed, the fine sight of a dozen other skipjacks: sleek, low, and sloop-rigged, with sharp clipper bows.

"Heave, windward!" At Wadie's command, crew members threw one of *Sigsbee*'s two dredges overboard. When the pass over the bed was completed, a few minutes later, a mechanical winder brought the dredge up. With a scrape of metal its cargo of Bay bottom crashed on deck. Deckhands bent over and nimbly culled oysters from pounds of mud, shell, and rock. In big handloads, the crew swept the debris overboard. A shovel tightened the catch into a small pile.

"What a pitiful bunch of oysters," Wadie sighed, glancing over. Then, with one hand on the wheel and one on his coffee mug, he brought *Sigsbee* around for the next run. The scene was like a dance. Just yards apart, the skipjacks made parallel passes. Back and forth, back and forth. The names on the gilded trail boards—*Stanley Norman,*

Kathryn, Martha Lewis—gained a human quality. Crews bantered across the water. The wind died down, but the mood stayed expansive. The numbing cold and the dangerous storms that winter would bring seemed hard to imagine on this sunny day.

But Wadie had bad news for his crew. Oysters were so scarce, he told them all, that he would have to start taking *Sigsbee* 30 miles up the Bay, for a week at a time, to work different beds. "To make a living this winter," he said, "we're going to have to leave home. That's something I've never done in 25 years of dredging." The local beds were overworked, Wadie told me. He also mentioned a new, more efficient way being used by some to get the dwindling numbers of oysters.

In this new method, commercial divers gather oysters from the bottom of the Bay. Diving is so efficient, according to Laura Era, of Cambridge, Maryland, that some people think it will deplete the oyster beds. Laura herself was something of a novelty on the Bay. Before I met her, I hadn't seen any women working on the water. But every day, Laura pins her long blonde hair up and, with her husband, Richard, harvests oysters by tonging on the Choptank River. She told me about other women who were starting to follow the water—just one example of the changes I saw taking place around the Chesapeake.

In Wicomico Church, Virginia, I met Driscoll Pitman, who, as his forebears did, farms near the mouth of the Potomac River. He told me about the waterfront cropland being sold to build pleasure-boat marinas. In Lloyds, Maryland, there was Jim Richardson, the last in a long family line of master boatbuilders. He spoke of the once rich variety in the Bay's native boats, a variety that has largely given way to standardized designs. On the other hand, Jim was building a bugeye, a type of workboat that hasn't sailed commercially in decades: On the Chesapeake, just as you see new ways marching in, you blink and find that the region's deep stability is all around.

"This is an outpost of what's been," said one Eastern Shore matron as she gestured around the grounds of her lovely old estate. Along with the Bay's tidy fishing villages, the many stately manors of the Chesapeake—in Maryland's Talbot County and Virginia's Northern Neck especially—provide a touch of timelessness. Many remain in the hands of the families who built them.

One such place is Wye House, on the Wye River near the city of Easton, Maryland. Elizabeth Lloyd Schiller greeted me in its great foyer. "I'm the ninth generation here," she said, "and members of the tenth have been here also." As we walked through the rooms, she paused before the portraits of several earlier residents, speaking of them with such familiarity that she might have been performing introductions. On the headstones in the graveyard, the names of Maryland's oldest families intertwined like ancient vines.

In her 80s, Elizabeth Schiller still manages Wye House's 850 cultivated acres. When I visited, she was about to leave for a week of opera-going in Baltimore. We chatted in a sun-filled parlor. "We still have a great many weddings and funerals here," she said. "Relatives will call and say that they'd like their baby to be christened here. It's always the same christening bowl. You know, everyone who comes here has a feeling that I always have, a feeling of continuity. This place has gone on and on. It gives you a feeling of, maybe, security."

"You can't help but live in the past here," says a pensive Elizabeth Lloyd Schiller. "The past is so interesting and so very colorful." At home at Wye House, she represents the ninth generation of Maryland's Lloyd family, whose members have inhabited the sprawling Eastern Shore estate since 1663. Relatives dispersed to far-flung parts still return for weddings, funerals, and christenings in heirloom-filled parlors. Below, James Boulden, butler at Wye House for 21 years, lights candles at a setting for six. An early resident, in the uniform of the Coldstream Guards, appears in a portrait by American artist Benjamin West.

Her smooth skin glowed as Elizabeth, erect in her wing chair, spoke quietly. "We use the same big key now that Mrs. Lloyd, my grandmother, used to lock out the Union soldiers during the Civil War," she told me. "I touch the same things that people did in the 1700s. I have letters of the Mrs. Lloyds who have lived here that could have been written by women of any generation."

The whole area around Wye House is a fabled land of pleasant living. Its quaint towns—St. Michaels, Oxford—have acquired cachet for yachtsmen and become well known to tourists. Across the Bay, in the Virginia Tidewater area, once elegant Reedville is now known only as the home of the menhaden fishing fleet. There I met a woman who has the same gentle poise as Elizabeth Schiller, but a different story to tell.

The sign in the yard of the little house read: "Martha's Cookbooks." Inside, Martha Drummond Curry sported a T-shirt with the same message. Surrounded by framed photographs and mementos from her son's Army service, Martha told me that when her mother left them as children, she and her siblings went to live with relatives. "We were poor but they weren't. We had to cut all the wood, slop the hogs, feed the turkeys. We lived like Cinderella."

Martha ran away and lived in the woods; eventually she met the man she married. "My husband always did hunt," she said. "I'd fix up what he came back with. And we'd get those fish—those menhaden that other people wouldn't eat—and I'd cook them a hundred different ways. Hard times got me interested in cooking.

"I didn't have enough money to finish school, but that didn't

matter. I had to *make* something of my life." Before dawn she left home to work as a crab picker, then returned to send her son off to school. Then she left again to put in time at tomato canneries and fish processing plants. In the summer, she followed her husband and the menhaden fleet to Long Island, where she picked beans and shucked scallops. Slowly, she put her recipes together. The first printing of *Martha's Cooking Seafood* has sold out; Martha's venison cookbook is doing well, too. They had been flawlessly printed and bound on Martha's own equipment. Martha has also appeared on local television to demonstrate her cooking. But that wasn't enough: "If I can just scrape together the money, I'll open my own restaurant."

The real proof, so to speak, was in the pudding. Martha led me into her kitchen, set a cast-iron skillet on the stove, and whipped up some of the best crab cakes anywhere—heavenly concoctions of pure crabmeat, mayonnaise, mustard, and spices. As we sat there enjoying them, she commented, "No matter what becomes of me, if someone stops in, I can always give them a meal—and feel good about it."

A spirit of generosity pervades Bay country. Everywhere I went, doors opened, help was offered, and invitations were extended. Typical of that spirit was an incident that occurred after a service I attended at the African Methodist Episcopal Church in Eastville, Virginia. As I was getting into my car, a teenage boy came up and said, all in one breath, "You have a flat tire and I'll change it for you." The goodwill goes out to friends, family, and strangers alike. At the same church in Eastville, in an area of high unemployment, the altar was surrounded by mounds of vegetables and canned goods—Thanksgiving offerings to less fortunate neighbors.

Throughout the region there is also a natural grace about even the most mundane daily routines. I saw it in the split-second greeting that backroads drivers always exchange. I saw that grace in the way 25-year-old Pam Page shucked oysters for a living. I also heard it in her description of how she won the national oyster shucking

Sunset gleams from the window of a Tangier Island home; its gabled roof and simple frame construction typify Bay architecture. Nearby, a diminutive Halloween spirit offers a ghostly grin beneath a jaunty souvenir hat.

FOLLOWING PAGES: Ribbons of water trace a marshy course across Tangier Island, where homes ride narrow ridgetop crests.

championship: "I had rhythm with me. I was just moving back and forth and smiling the whole time."

Grace, rhythm, and symmetry: They were overhead with the migrating geese. They were in the decoys carved in every backyard shed. They were, especially, in the watermen's work—in the dip and rise of crabbers or the heave and haul of dredgers. They were in the cycles within cycles of life on the vulnerable, bountiful Bay.

An Endless Expanse

The Prairie and Badlands

By SUZANNE VENINO

Photographs by JIM BRANDENBURG

Amber waves of grain ripple under sunny skies on a wheat farm in eastern Nebraska. A century and a half ago, many people deemed the vast midwestern prairie a wasteland. Gradually the prairie yielded to the plows of homesteaders, growing into one of the most productive agricultural regions in the world. Yet pockets of virgin grasslands remain, and the barren badlands continue to cast their spell of untamed grandeur.

# of Earth and Sky

A covered wagon creaks and sways across a vast, treeless landscape. Pots and pans clang against the sideboards, and children laugh as they run alongside. This is a family of homesteaders, heading west to stake a claim and start a new life. The place is the prairie. The time, less than a century ago.

Settlers like these who ventured into this barren frontier often had little more than a willing spirit and a wagonful of possessions. With few trees or rocks for building materials, many pioneers built their homes of the earth, stacking up layers of sod sliced from the prairie. These houses provided a sturdy shelter on the windswept plains, and the thick walls kept the houses warm in winter and cool in summer.

"We lived in a two-room sod house near Buffalo Creek, in North Dakota," said Pearl Trotter, a petite woman of 88 with white hair and a kind face that broke into a road map of wrinkles with each smile. "We papered the inside of the roof with newspapers to keep the dirt from falling down. The inside walls were plastered and whitewashed, and we had a board floor. There were curtains at the windows—glass windows that my folks ordered from back East. And my mother always kept the house full of plants. Begonias, I remember mostly."

Pearl's family moved from the sod house when she was a child. For the past 67 years Pearl has lived in a hand-hewn log cabin nestled among the buttes of the North Dakota badlands. As we sipped iced tea in her kitchen she told me of growing up on the frontier. She spoke of digging coal out of the hillsides and gathering wild fruit, of fighting prairie fires and watching the northern lights in a winter sky. She spoke of hard work and self-reliance, of an independent spirit and the need for neighbors in order to survive in this rugged land. She spoke of the good times, of sing-alongs, sleigh rides, and dancing till dawn to the sound of a fiddle. She told me of the closeness she felt for the land and of her love of the outdoors.

As Pearl talked she described a life I had read about in page after page of pioneer diaries. And she painted a portrait of the people I would meet as I traveled across the prairie. In a span of seven weeks I traveled more than 5,000 miles through North and South Dakota and parts of Nebraska, Iowa, and Minnesota. Outlined on a map, this region forms a rectangle, though it's an arbitrary boundary considering nearly all of the Midwest was once prairie. But within this area lies a sampler of prairie life, both past and present.

While there I danced at an Indian powwow and wrestled calves at a calf branding. I drove past miles of cornfields, wheatfields, and open range. I tramped across patches of virgin prairie bursting with wild flowers, and I gazed upon the beauty of the badlands, areas of extreme erosion where rivers have carved the land into a fantasy scene of spires, buttes, pinnacles, and plateaus.

Etched from the prairie by the wanderings of the Little Missouri River, the North Dakota badlands cover a thousand square miles in the southwestern part of the state. Sioux Indians called the area *mako sica*—land bad—because of the difficulty of traveling over the contorted terrain. French fur trappers, the first white men to enter the region, called it *les mauvaises terres à traverser*—the bad lands to cross. Despite the negative name, the spectacle of the badlands has captured the hearts of many.

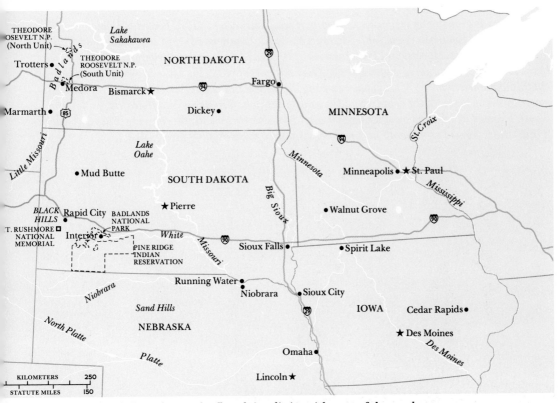

Gently rolling hills and pancake-flat plains distinguish most of the northern prairie. Exceptions include the Black Hills of South Dakota, which rise some 3,500 feet above the plains, and the badlands—gnarled terrain that formed over millennia as meandering rivers eroded away the prairie.

In 1883 a young politician from New York came west to hunt bison. Theodore Roosevelt quickly fell in love with the Little Missouri badlands. He bought 400 head of cattle and a partnership in a ranch, and he returned the following year. The western Dakota Territory was raw and rugged, peopled mostly by hardened cowhands. They laughed at this Eastern dude, who didn't drink or swear and who wore funny glasses. They called him Ole Four-Eyes. But they grew to respect Roosevelt for his spirit and determination.

Today a 110-square-mile park bears his name. Headquarters of the Theodore Roosevelt National Park is in Medora, a town of 91 year-round residents that swells to a daily population of more than 3,000 during the peak summer season. Visitors come by car, camper, motorcycle, and by the busload. Many take the loop drive through the park, for 36 miles of paved road have made the "bad lands to cross" an easy place to visit. An even better way to see the park is on horseback.

On a cool, misty morning I headed out with Micki Hellickson, chief park interpreter. We rode down steep draws shaded by stands of green ash. We crossed open areas tinged with the blue-gray of sagebrush and a filigree of yellow sweet clover. At the edge of the Big Plateau we looked down upon the Little Missouri River, a shallow, winding ribbon of water. "It's hard to *(Continued on page 70)*

65

"The country is growing on me, more and more; it has a curious, fantastic beauty of its own. . . ." So wrote Theodore Roosevelt of the Little Missouri badlands, where he ranched in the late 1880s. Today the Theodore Roosevelt National Park preserves 110 square miles of this "grimly picturesque" area in the southwestern corner of North Dakota. Over millions of years, the Little Missouri River (below) cut through ancient layers of sediments, carving the prairie into an outlandish terrain. Wind and water continue to sculpt the details. Sudden rainstorms etch steep slopes into fluted ridges (lower right). Exposed by constant weathering of the soft badlands' sediments, the round rock at right, called a concretion, formed as minerals accumulated around a fossil or other foreign body.

68

Dressed in garb of days gone by, five-year-old Tesa Rode and her brother, Lucas, age three, capture the frontier spirit at the 1982 centennial celebration in Dickey, North Dakota. The citizens of Dickey, population 74, played host to a three-day birthday festival complete with contests, a high school reunion, and dancing on Main Street. At left, local politicians wave to onlookers during the centennial parade. Community pride stands tall in prairie towns, even in the one-man town of Trotters, North Dakota, where, at lower left, Leonard Hall—storekeeper, gas station attendant, and postmaster for area ranchers—lowers the town flag at sunset.

believe that the Little Missouri did much of this," said Micki with a sweep of her arm, "but it did.

"Starting about 60 million years ago, ancient rivers deposited layers of sand, silt, and other sediments, and vast quantities of ash settled here from volcanic eruptions to the west," Micki explained. "About two million years ago the Little Missouri and its tributaries started cutting through the soft strata, creating the badlands you now see."

All through the badlands the layers of sediment stand out as if someone had colored them with crayons—blue, tan, brown, black, orange. "The orange is scoria," said Micki, "a clay baked hard and bricklike when adjacent seams of lignite caught fire, as sometimes happens when lightning sets the grasslands aflame."

Some 350 billion tons of lignite, a low-grade coal, lie buried in western North Dakota, where it has been mined for nearly a century. Oil too has been discovered here, and in recent years an oil boom has greatly affected the area surrounding the park. "There are mixed feelings about the coal and oil development," said Micki. "There is a concern about the impact. Right now companies are applying for waivers on air pollution limits. Yet development also means jobs and money. These aren't the good old days any more. This country is changing."

The northern prairie has undergone dramatic changes in recent history. In 1803 the United States bought most of the land from France as part of the Louisiana Purchase. Until the mid-1800s, though, few whites had settled here, mostly fur trappers and traders who lived in relative peace among the Indians.

With the Homestead Act of 1862, Congress opened the area for settlement. Any person 21 or older could obtain 160 acres of land if he would farm 20 acres and live there for five years. Homesteaders came from all over the United States and from Europe, too—from Sweden, Norway, Germany, and Russia. For the land was free.

Settling the fertile lands to the east first and gradually fanning westward across the Missouri River, the homesteaders sparked a population boom. Towns sprang up. Churches and schools were built, and railroads crisscrossed the prairie. From 1870 to 1920 the population of the Dakotas increased nearly tenfold. Nevertheless the northern prairie is still a sparsely populated agricultural area where livestock outnumber people. Recently there has been a population decrease, as young people leave rural areas for greater job opportunities in larger towns and cities. The cities grow while the small towns are dying.

"If this town isn't dead yet, it's sure laid out nice," said Merle Clark as he tucked a pinch of Skoal tobacco under his lip. A rancher and auctioneer, Merle told me the history of Marmarth, North Dakota, as we walked among the remains of a roundhouse where railroad crews once serviced steam locomotives.

"In 1908 there was only a tent town here. Then the railroad came through, and the town blossomed overnight. By 1914 there was a population of about 2,400." Shops and saloons lined Main Street. There were three hotels and three banks. For the opening of the opera house, ladies ordered ball gowns from Chicago. Six passenger trains stopped daily. Marmarth was a bustling prairie town. "The decline started in the 1950s," Merle continued, "when the railroads switched from coal-fired steam to diesel and no longer needed large crews." Passenger service ended in the '60s. Today even the freight train no longer stops.

The population of Marmarth has dwindled to fewer than 250. The vacant buildings on Main Street are either boarded up or tumbling down. There's one bar, a cafe, and the Mystic Theater. In 1976 the Marmarth Historical Society and a crew of volunteers restored the old theater, a silent-movie house built in 1914. But they did more than just return the building to the splendor of its gilt trim and red-velvet wallpaper—they brought the theater back to life. "The cast is mostly ranchers and farmers," said Delight Stottlemyer, the director. "Work comes first, so we schedule shows around chores. We usually do a play in the spring, after calving and before seeding."

Performing to sell-out crowds, they put on several productions a year—from vaudeville reviews to melodramas to full-scale musicals. As Frederic "Fritz" Bruggeman, the one-man orchestra, warmed up the piano keys, the curtains opened and I sat back to enjoy a rollicking evening of singing, dancing, and comedy routines. The theater resounded with laughter and applause. And at the end, the audience stood to join the cast in singing "God Bless America."

After the performance, at a potluck supper on stage-turned-buffet, I spoke with members of the cast. Over the years the original cast of 30 has grown into a theater group of about 120 members. To attend rehearsals three times a week some members drive more than 130

Home sweet homestead: The sod house provided a rough but durable first home for many settlers starting a new life on the plains. A prairie family built this sod dugout into the side of a hill in 1909 near Interior, South Dakota.

SUZANNE VENINO

miles round trip on winding, unpaved roads. "It takes a lot of dedication," said one member, "and a lot of gasoline."

West of the Missouri River the farms and ranches are few, and I quickly learned that driving long distances is a fact of life. This country is *big*. The prairie spreads out before you, cresting in gentle hills that roll toward the horizon. There's a subtle beauty in this endless expanse of earth and sky. It inspires a feeling of *(Continued on page 78)*

Small, shallow ponds dimple tilled fields on a North Dakota farm in the prairie pothole region. The area covers a wide swath from central Canada through the eastern Dakotas and into western Minnesota. As the last of the Ice Age glaciers receded northward, large blocks of melting ice left thousands of depressions that later filled with water. These fertile pothole marshes, called sloughs, proffer food and nesting cover for migrating waterfowl. Situated on one of the three major North American flyways, the prairie pothole region supports the highest concentration of breeding waterfowl in the U. S.

Racing across the water, two western grebes perform an elaborate mating dance known as "rushing" (right). Dependent on the marsh habitat for breeding, grebes build their nests on water. In the shallows the birds pile up low mounds of decaying vegetation; in deeper water they anchor floating nests to reeds. Below, a single pied-billed grebe egg rests in an isolated nest; at lower right, a horned grebe guards its clutch.

PAGES 76-77: Windblown grasses and green algae pattern a pothole marsh. Flying low, water birds search for insects and small fish.

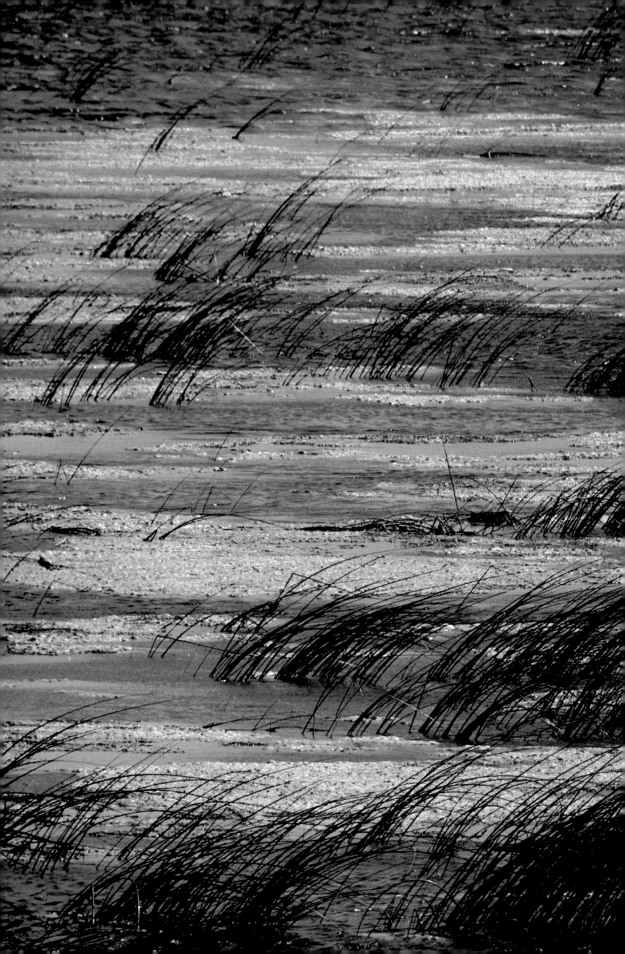

freedom. "I love the wide open spaces," a rancher said to me. "In a city I can't see. I feel like a caged stallion."

Virgin prairie once stretched from the Gulf of Mexico into Canada, and from the Rocky Mountains to the forests of Illinois. Along the eastern portion of this area, where the soil is fertile and rainfall abundant, stood the tallgrass prairie. Plowed under by sodbusters, it grew into the corn belt. The thinner soils and semiarid climate to the west support shortgrass prairie, used as a graze for livestock. In between is the mid- or mixed-grass prairie, which is grazed as well as farmed for wheat and other small grains. Conservationists estimate that only one percent of the original tallgrass prairie remains. Approximately 50 percent of the mixed- and shortgrass prairies still exist, for while farming destroys the native grasses, grazing does not.

The prairie is a rich tapestry of grasses, wild flowers, and other plants. Throughout the growing season flowers bloom in a showy parade of color. Grasses, though, dominate the prairie biome. Hardy perennials, the native grasses have deep, extensive root systems that can withstand fires, sub-zero winters, and years of drought.

A huge community of wildlife once lived on the grasslands. Most of the large, conspicuous animals have been hunted to extinction or greatly reduced in numbers. The grizzly bear and the wolf no longer roam the plains; elk and bighorn sheep exist only where reintroduced. Other animals have suffered from loss of habitat. The surviving

wildlife tends to live close to the ground or burrow beneath it—animals such as jackrabbits, gophers, foxes, coyotes, ground-nesting birds, snakes, and insects. One study estimates that within one square mile of prairie there are more than 650 million insects!

To discover the secrets of the prairie, you must look closely. A tiny spider climbs a stalk of needlegrass. Butterflies chase one another in flitting circles. The grape-size buffalo bean, a legume that tastes like raw peas, grows on a ground-clinging vine. Many farmers and ranchers showed me fossils, along with arrowheads and other artifacts they had found in their fields. On his ranch north of Mud Butte, South Dakota, Jennings Floden found a tyrannosaur.

Scientists say that 65 million years ago, during the Age of Reptiles, this area of shortgrass prairie was a steamy subtropical swamp. Stalking the cypress marshes, *Tyrannosaurus rex*—the King Tyrant Lizard—stood 16 feet tall, measured 44 feet long, and weighed as much as 8 tons—the largest meat-eater ever to walk the earth.

As a young boy Jennings had often seen the darkened bone poking out of a steep-sided butte. When a paleontologist from a local college came to take a look, he discovered a daggerlike tooth 5½ inches long. A tyrannosaur! Only five other of these skeletons have ever been found. The Flodens and a small group of friends helped paleontologists excavate the dinosaur, sometimes cutting hay or tending livestock at night so they could work at the dig during the day. When the time came to remove the four-foot-long skull from its ancient grave, journalists and television crews from across the country recorded the event. Now when people ask the Flodens what they raise on their ranch, they reply, "Oh, cattle and sheep . . . and dinosaurs."

*I*t was a bluebird-bright morning when I pointed my car in the direction of the South Dakota badlands. An ominous gray thunderhead began building in the west, mushrooming miles high in the sky. It dropped a black curtain of rain as it passed overhead, and then the sun shone again. The only evidence of the sudden storm was my newly washed car and the fresh, pungent odor of ozone.

In the distance the forested heights of the Black Hills rose from the prairie. A gold rush drew swarms of prospectors to the Black Hills in the late 1800s. Today the Homestake Mine is the most productive gold mine in the Western Hemisphere, and the Black Hills have become the mother lode of the South Dakota tourist industry. Each year nearly two and a half million people visit the Hills' campsites, ski slopes, and historic attractions, such as Mount Rushmore. In their hurry to get to the Black Hills, many vacationers drive right by Exits 10 and 11 on Interstate 90. It is too bad, for a slight detour off the highway leads to a realm of unimagined sights.

The badlands of South Dakota are often described as a moonscape, and indeed they look like something out of science fiction. Fanciful formations conjure images of giant sand castles, cathedrals, or armies of soldiers frozen in time. It's a moody landscape that changes its look with the hours of the day: gentle in the pink glow of morning, harsh and unforgiving at midday, mysterious in the soft shadows of dusk before darkness transforms the badlands into an eerie, haunting world. The eroding action of the White River created these badlands as it washed away layers of sediment deposited over millions of years. Wind and water continually weather away *(Continued on page 85)*

Feeding time: A young white pelican, quick-growing but slow to mature, pokes its head into its parent's gullet for a meal of fish (left). An American bittern (right) hides among marsh grasses by standing still in a head-up position.

Wings spread for a landing, a ferruginous hawk returns to its nest of downy chicks. With few trees available on the prairie, ferruginous hawks often build their nests on the ground. Both parents tend the young, bringing food to the edge of the nest where they tear it up and drop it into waiting mouths. Feeding primarily on rodents, ferruginous hawks swoop down from the sky and capture live prey with their sharp talons. Black-tailed prairie dogs, ever-alert to hawks soaring overhead, live in large towns on the open prairie, where natural enemies abound. If danger approaches, these rabbit-size rodents bark out an alarm and run for the safety of their burrows. A high-pitched yip with head thrown back (right) signals all clear. At far right, a badger feeds on a prairie dog it dug out of a burrow.

*Grassy plateaus fall away to weather-scarred hills in
Badlands National Park, South Dakota. Banded layers
of sand, silt, clay, and volcanic ash show distinctly in the
wrinkled landscape. "You can read the history of the
badlands through the layers of sediments," says Nick
Raymond, a geologist with the U. S. Geological Survey.
Above, Raymond searches for mineral samples in a remote
area of the park most easily accessible by helicopter. "We
are always discovering new information," he says.*

the crumbly surface, sculpturing the landscape and revealing the scattered bones and teeth of long-extinct animals.

The jumbled terrain covers an area about a hundred miles long by fifty miles wide; 243,000 acres of the most spectacular scenery are preserved in the Badlands National Park. A million people a year drive through the park, but in the designated wilderness areas, motorized vehicles are prohibited. District ranger Mike Glass and I went instead by four-legged horse power.

We left from Sage Creek Basin, lush with grasses, cottonwood trees, and waist-high sunflowers. Quickly, though, the landscape changed to a desolate, thirsty world nearly void of vegetation. Prickly pear cactus and withered clumps of sagebrush clung to the parched earth. Sunflowers, here only inches tall, added a faint hint of color.

As we topped a low hill, another hill came into view, and another—a seemingly unending procession. There was not a tree in sight to provide relief from the sun's glare. It was hot and dusty. I felt like a pioneer. Suddenly a small herd of pronghorns dashed by, their tails raised in alert, revealing white rump patches. Fleet and graceful, pronghorns are the fastest land animals in North America. Disappearing behind a hill, they looked as if they were gliding on wheels.

After several hours of riding we reached the "wall," the precipitous 250-foot cliff where the prairie gives way to the badlands in a maze of fluted ridges. By wriggling up close to the wall, we found a sliver of shade where we sat to eat lunch. The only sound was the cooing of mourning doves on the cliffs above.

The yips and squeaks from a prairie dog town that we saw after lunch seemed a noisy contrast. Hundreds of plump sentries sat at burrow openings, alert for hawks, badgers, or other predators. As Mike and I approached, a string of high-pitched yips went up in a warning call. We must not have been too much of a threat, for the animated rodents continued nibbling on grasses or chasing one another in a comical run. In a flurry of feathers a burrowing owl flew out of the ground. These small birds live in prairie dog burrows, as do other denizens of the prairie: rattlesnakes and black widow spiders.

Several hundred yards away we saw something large and dark. Riding closer we could see it was a bison, a lone bull apart from the herd. Though bison is the correct name, the animals are more commonly referred to as buffalo. Bulls may stand six feet tall at the shoulders and weigh more than a ton. They are fast, agile, and dangerously unpredictable. When this one saw us he stood up, watching our movement, his tail raised in nervous excitement.

"If he charges, just follow me," said Mike.

"But I thought a buffalo could outrun a horse."

"Yep."

Fortunately, the buffalo simply trotted off, stopping occasionally to look back, as if to make sure we too were on our way. As many as 60 million buffalo once roamed North America. Today there are about

Signs of spring: Baby horned larks hatch and pasqueflowers bloom soon after the snow melts on the prairie. The short-lived blossoms of pasqueflowers die back to leave the wispy tendrils (right) that give this plant its other name—prairie smoke.

55,000; many are raised for their beef-like meat, while others live protected in parklands. "We have 300 to 350 buffalo here in Badlands National Park," said Mike. "If the herd gets much bigger than that they wander out of the park. Once every three years or so we round 'em up and give the surplus to the Pine Ridge Indian Reservation."

Indian reservations are scattered throughout the northern prairie. South of Badlands National Park—in fact, overlapping the lower

Native pronghorns stand alert under lowering skies on the open range of North Dakota. Small herds still roam the prairie, though greatly reduced in number over the past century. Today domestic cattle dominate the grasslands.

portion of the park—lies the Pine Ridge Reservation, home of the Oglala Sioux. Though the life of the Sioux has changed dramatically since they ruled the plains, a back-to-roots movement has kindled a renewed interest in their cultural heritage. For example, high school and elementary students now study their native language; until the 1940s it was illegal to teach or even speak the Sioux language in reservation schools. Elective courses offer classes in Sioux history and philosophy. Clubs meet after school to learn traditional music and dance.

"Just a few years ago teenagers went off to rock and roll dances while the adults attended the tribe's powwows," said Tony Apple, a Sioux who lives on the reservation and works for the park as a ranger. "Now the young people powwow too and participate with pride."

In the summer there's a community powwow just about every weekend. And just about every weekend there's also a rodeo. They come in all shapes and sizes, from "little britches" rodeos for youngsters to "old-timer" rodeos for more mature cowboys. Sitting in a saddle is second nature to people in ranch country. They learn to ride almost as soon as they learn to walk. Most ranches and farms have a couple of saddle horses, a snowmobile for winter range work, and—of course—a pickup truck.

"Kinda warm today," I said to Austin Sybrant as I climbed into his pickup. "Darn right hot," he replied.

Austin, a retired rancher, and his daughter, Ila Mae, had offered to show me their corner of the world in the Sand Hills of northern Nebraska. The Sand Hills are actually a vast system of dunes—the most extensive in the Western Hemisphere—formed several thousand years ago when winds carried the sands of dry riverbeds and molded them into an expanse of undulating hills. A luxuriant growth of mixed-grass prairie makes the area premium ranchland.

Every once in a while we passed a large, square grove of trees. "Tree claims," said Austin. "The only trees here are the ones that someone planted. A homesteader could get an extra 160 acres of land if he planted ten acres of trees."

As we drove along unpaved county roads trailing plumes of dust, I asked Austin about his family and how he came to live here. "My grandfather homesteaded here in 1886. He'd heard there was land available and money to be made. So he and his family came out from Pennsylvania, settled here, and founded the Sybrant community."

And community it is. It's not a town—there's no post office or police department. It's simply a small, close-knit group of ranchers and farmers who attend the same church and send their children to the same school. "My grandfather helped build the first school here, a one-room sod building. My pop went to school there," Austin went on as he pushed back his Stetson. "Later it was replaced by a frame schoolhouse. That's where I went. I rode a horse to school. There was a barn out back big enough for 14 horses."

The Sybrant School was rebuilt once more. Austin's children attended the school, and now his grandchildren go there. But there's no longer a barn for horses; instead, there are swings and monkeybars, a basketball court, and an outhouse still used if the school's pipes freeze in winter. Sixteen students attend the one-room school, kindergarten through eighth grade. The day I paid a visit the children were excited and fidgety, but on best behavior for their guest.

I asked 12-year-old Jeff Sybrant how he gets to school in the morning. "I drive," he answered, "and pick up a cousin along the way." Next year when Jeff graduates he'll go to high school 20 miles away in the town of Bassett. Students from rural areas often drive to school on special permits or board in town during the week and go home on weekends. Sometimes the whole family may move to town while the father commutes to the country.

Leaving the Sand Hills, I traveled northward to the Missouri River, once a major highway for Indians, explorers, and settlers. The upper Missouri is now a series of dammed lakes, its waters impounded for flood control as well as for irrigation and electricity. Lakes Oahe and Sakakawea are the largest man-made lakes in the United States and on weekends are busy with sailboats, water-skiers, and fishermen casting for walleyed pike. Along a brief stretch of the river that still runs free, I crossed the Missouri in a paddle-wheel ferry.

"Except for a period during World War II, there's been a paddle-wheel ferry here since 1864," said Captain Mickey May. "The first one was a wooden raft that was powered by two horses on a treadwheel."

With several cars on deck, the ferry left Niobrara, Nebraska, and churned across the river past chalk cliffs mottled with the mud nests of cliff swallows. "This part of the river looks much as it did when Lewis and Clark and the Corps of Discovery came up in flat-bottomed keelboats," Mickey said. As we docked at Running Water, South Dakota, the scenery looked far different from the wilderness Lewis and Clark encountered. Fields of crops checkerboarded the countryside. Driving down the road, I passed half a dozen farms within a few miles.

East of the Missouri River the population is denser. Towns are closer together. The climate is more humid, better suited to farming. And unlike the sedimentary soils west of the river, the soil here was formed during the Ice Age as advancing ice sheets ground rock into a rich glacial till. Here is found the corn belt—miles and miles of green fields where tallgrass prairie once grew. Today only remnants of virgin tallgrass are found along railroad right-of-ways, in pioneer cemeteries, and in small, preserved pockets of prairie.

In the northwestern corner of Iowa, near Spirit Lake, I visited Cayler Prairie, 160 acres of virgin grassland preserved by the state as a "botanical monument." A kaleidoscope of color, it seemed more garden than prairie: lacy white blooms of western yarrow, delicate purples of horsemint, bright yellows of coneflowers and black-eyed Susans, the blushing pink of prairie roses.

Big bluestem, the skyscraper of prairie grasses, was said to grow taller than a man on a horse. It was over my head when I stopped at Wahpeton Prairie in Walnut Grove, Minnesota. As a child, Laura Ingalls Wilder, author of *Little House on the Prairie*, lived nearby in a sod house and probably played here.

Eighty acres of native tallgrass, Wahpeton Prairie is owned by the Nature Conservancy, a private organization that in recent years has set aside more than 100,000 acres of midwestern prairie for preservation and research. Such unplowed, untamed areas are living laboratories for the study of prairie ecology, offering a better understanding of the interlocking web of plant and animal life that makes up the prairie.

The prairie is many things. It's a shaggy carpet of grass swaying with the ever present rhythms of the wind. It is endless vistas, a hillside of sego lilies. It is the clicks and chirps of a chorus of insects.

The prairie is a part of our national heritage. A rugged frontier braved and settled by a hardy, steadfast people who survived the hard times when others packed up and left. They built a life on the prairie, a good life. And they passed it down through generations. Whenever I asked people why they live here, the answer was simple, and always the same: Because it's home.

In the prairie, roots grow deep.

Keeping the old ways alive, Frank Fool's Crow, 95, invokes healing powers and conducts sacred tribal rites as medicine man and ceremonial chief for the Oglala Sioux of the Pine Ridge Indian Reservation, in South Dakota.

PAGES 90-91: Bison nuzzle through snow to graze in winter. In the distance rise buttes of the South Dakota badlands—a realm of desolate beauty.

'The Last Place on
The Upper Peninsula

By MARY ANN HARRELL

Photographs by LOWELL GEORGIA

*Winter prelude on Michigan's remote Upper
Peninsula: David Trudell of Stambaugh
pauses in his task of building his woodpile to a
cold-weather supply of 20 to 30 cords. Trudell,
who spent 25 of his 73 years as an iron miner,
died in the spring of 1983. "He was an
outdoorsman," says his wife. "He loved
hunting and fishing." Mrs. Trudell sums up
life in this proud and isolated region: "Our
family loves it. People help one another here."*

Earth'

"*The* Last Place on Earth." The sign on the old store wall by U. S. 41 seemed inevitable. All through Michigan's Upper Peninsula runs a sense of the ultimate outpost, the most distant community, the limit of human things. "This is not the edge of the world," Bruce Johanson of Ontonagon told me, "but you can see it from here."

"I know," I exclaimed. "I already have." A few days in the U.P. had given me an addiction to Lake Superior, a devotion I never expected to feel for water too cold to swim in. On an August afternoon, I had found my way from Ironwood out a narrow two-lane road that curved toward sundown, to a park at Little Girls Point. I stopped in a grove of white birches, jumped out into brilliant sun, and stared out over the water: sky blue at the zenith but milk-white at the horizon, lake steel-hued and ax-sharp at its rim. I seemed to be gazing not toward the edge of the world, but the edge of the universe.

As a little girl in North Carolina, I dreamed of seeing "real" north country someday, the "dark and gloomy" forest of *Hiawatha*. Later, Hemingway's short stories brought a modern overlay to Longfellow's poetic descriptions, and friends from Lower Michigan told me about the remote portion of their state that is the U.P. "We thought of it as friendly, but up there alone, like Canada," said one. "We learned to draw our state in school," said another, "but just the lower 'mitten' "—a footnote to the U.P. lament that "They leave us off the maps."

On a proper map, the U.P. blocks Lake Superior—the Big Lake— from Lake Michigan, with Lake Huron off its southeastern tip. It has a ragged shape, like a slab of its native copper, and 1,074 miles of shoreline. It holds 16,882 square miles of land, mainly wooded; about 320,000 people, many unemployed; scattered talk of secession and statehood; and character worthy of an independent planet.

The authentic U.P. individual, or Yooper, expects hardship, if only from winter, and meets it staunchly. I heard of a little boy with a broken tooth, forced to wait for dental help. "He'll tough it out," said his father. "He's a real Yooper." The Yooper is a housewife braiding rugs for her home out of plastic bread wrappers. Or a retired miner, undaunted by cancer, cutting wood for the winter. Or a young woman in labor, walking a mile over the snow to the highway where the family pickup is waiting.

In keeping with their hard life, the people of the U.P. possess a determined pride. "Life is standing tall today, like these trees." The voice of moderator Billy Blackwell rang through the ritual enclosure on a July morning. Indians from as far away as Oklahoma had come to the Keweenaw Bay Tribal Center for a conference on spiritual traditions, and guests were welcome. Sunlight gleamed through leaves that keep the freshness of spring through the fleeting northern summer. Smoke curled from "the sacred fire made with flint . . . which the Creator gave us. The Creator will be watching, the plant life will be watching. . . ."

Elders gave everyone a portion of tobacco for an offering. A small boy scampered to the fire with his. Others dropped it gravely into the flame. One young man held it up to the four directions. An invocation, in Chippewa then in English, called on four great *manitos,* the spirits of the East, the South, the West, the North, "to give us a blessing . . . to look upon us in a good way." Even when I caught only the music of Chippewa, the speakers' eloquence held me.

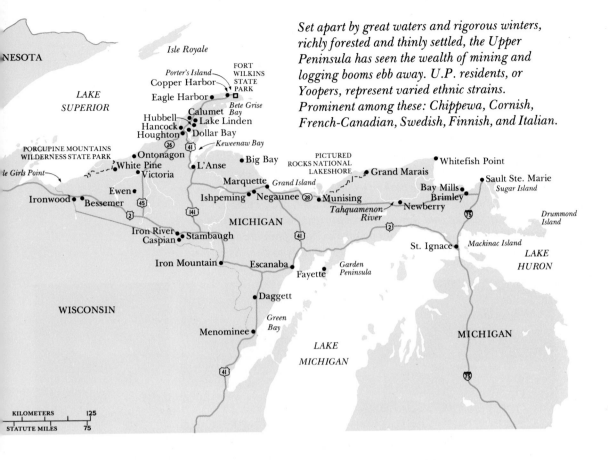

Set apart by great waters and rigorous winters, richly forested and thinly settled, the Upper Peninsula has seen the wealth of mining and logging booms ebb away. U.P. residents, or Yoopers, represent varied ethnic strains. Prominent among these: Chippewa, Cornish, French-Canadian, Swedish, Finnish, and Italian.

No stereotype holds up well in the U.P. Father John Hascall, Chippewa spiritual leader and Roman Catholic priest, describes his own looks as Irish. I noticed blue-eyed blond children, and later caught the remark: "So many of us have married Finns and Swedes, it's hard to tell who is an Indian any more." The dark-haired young man guarding the fire wore a Mardi Gras T-shirt. The ladies of the lunch committee served venison and corn, doughnuts and sheetcake.

And the spiritual leaders spoke with authority, often from experience, of how to help those "hurt in their brains" by alcohol and other drugs. I never heard a better summary of life in this exacting country than this: ". . . the bad is so bad that the good is right up there with it."

In this harsh land, I found the good in some of the loveliest moments I have ever known, at well-publicized places and nameless ones. I remember daybreak in the Porcupine Mountains, with a heavy animal bolting away unseen, and mist playing over the ridges as the stars dimmed. Fog dissolving over the famous Pictured Rocks at midday. Lake Huron's waters gray-green under rainy skies at Drummond Island, or rose-white with reflected sunset as a new moon gained brightness and ground fog swathed the trunks of dark young conifers.

One weekend I joined the Boy Scouts. That is, I was odd-rookie-in with expert canoeists of Troop 202, Lake Linden/Hubbell, for a trip on the Big Lake. We gathered on a sandy beach at a cove called Cat Harbor: Attorney/Scoutmaster Jim Kliber, Scouts age 11 to 18, and three fathers, Dick Stuffle, Chuck Wicker, and my new-met cousin Reggie

Savoring one of the U.P.'s most famous vistas, hiker Katie Kyyhkynen of Duluth, Minnesota, gazes over the valley of the Little Carp River in the Porcupine Mountains Wilderness State Park, Michigan's largest.
Within the park lies Lake of the Clouds, a magnet for visitors. Getting up early to enjoy a sunrise in the "Porkies," the author may have almost met a bear. "I heard a noise," she says, "and something heavy running away." Since black bears roam the park's 58,000 acres of woodlands, trail-wise campers store food—and bury scraps—with care, just as they use prudence in tasting wild things. Below, at right, maple leaves frame a fly agaric mushroom, appealing but poisonous. Near park headquarters, the Presque Isle River (below, left) cascades on its way to Lake Superior.

ANNIE GRIFFITHS (OPPOSITE)

Harrell. The sky was overcast, but the swell a demure ripple. We nibbled tender raw "beach peas," and Chuck found a ripe thimbleberry, my first. Dimpled in texture, ripening from greenish white to pink to brilliant red, these berries yield a sweet freshness on the tongue.

Then we were gliding along, eastward, past a classic northland shore: evergreens tall above huge ice-battered boulders. The immense water lay empty. The recession had idled most of the big "thousand-footer" ore boats. Lakeside cabins, shielded by trees, appeared only as they came abeam. "See that black hose?" Jim Kliber called. "Hardly anybody sinks a well here. The water's so pure you pump it right out of the lake." We dipped it up at will, delicious, cold, and uncannily clear. "I've seen pure raw copper maybe 50 feet down," said Jim. "Pieces as big as this canoe. No way to get it up. It would weigh tons."

As early as seven thousand years ago, Indians of the region were taking that copper from sites on the Keweenaw Peninsula and Isle Royale. Copper for spearpoints and knives, axes and fishhooks, pendants and C-shaped bracelets. At the very sites of that Old Copper Culture, 19th-century miners sank their shafts. Copper for the Navy, to sheathe wooden hulls; copper for the newfangled telegraph.

Light rain dimpled the shallows to thimbleberry texture. We swung inshore past long, saurian rock ledges. White yarrow was blooming there, as well as golden wild flowers and dainty blue harebells. Wind from the lake suddenly blew cold, but we reached our campsite islet in a burst of sun. We had a silver hunter's pit to plunk stones into, woodsmoke to season supper. In various contexts I heard the Copper Country sound of astonishment, elated or grim: "Whuh!" For emphasis, "Holy whuh!" And the slish and bicker of water on rock.

We had a slow start next morning, but a fair breeze. Two canoes lashed together, with a tree-branch mast, made a fair pace under a poncho sail. We cruised among rocks orange with lichen, eased into a blowhole called the Devil's Washtub. We saw one bulk carrier "up-bound," westward, and five juvenile Canada geese trundling about on shore. We made Porter's Island off Copper Harbor in good time, for shore leave and saunas, gossip, staring out to sea.

When the Scouts paddled on to Bete Grise Bay, I patrolled the Copper Country ashore. I saw Fort Wilkins, built in 1844 to guard the miners from an Indian attack that never came, and now restored to five-star polish. Here served, so to speak, Pvt. John Ryan, whose offenses included "General Worthlessness." I lingered on Brockway Mountain, where Jim Kliber once set a personal record in downhill bike-braking while avoiding a collision with a bear. I saw pink-purple spires of fireweed along litter-free highways, rusting towers at long-idle mines, massifs of tailings in shrinking towns, marvelous lakeside vistas, empty roads in peak tourist season.

In this century, the bad for the U.P. comes from a depressed economy. From Whitefish Point to Ironwood, Eagle Harbor to St. Ignace, I saw buildings for sale, tumbledown farm structures, fading signs for derelict resorts. Rich in ore and wood and water, this has been boom-

Ripe and soft and juicy, a thimbleberry fits neatly on the picker's thumb, ready for boiling down into a much-prized U.P. delicacy, homemade thimbleberry jam.

and-bust country since the copper rush of the 1840s. Too often it has been bust, or slump. "We're *used* to recessions," people say today. "This has been a depressed area for years." "Ya sure, it's still the 1930s."

"Faith—I'll be using *that* word many times." At Houghton, Bill Veeser—William L. Veeser, senior vice president of the Upper Peninsula Power Company—gave a stubbornly optimistic summary of U.P. economics. The Copper Range Company has built a state-of-the-art refinery at White Pine because "they believe copper will be back up." The Cleveland-Cliffs Iron Company has put "huge sums" into beneficiation, processing ore into iron-rich pellets before shipment. "Forest products—the U.P.'s a garden that we're managing." Ten million acres, some 80 percent of which is commercial forest, are being managed for sustained yield. Bill named firms investing millions. Finally, tourism and recreation, down slightly in 1982, but "full of promise."

The office of UPPCO, like other buildings in Houghton and nearby Hancock, records the turn-of-the-century glories of mining wealth. I tracked boom times through the U.P. in grandiose commercial blocks, in county courthouses and city halls, in the stained glass of churches and mansions and saloons. Often, above ground-floor facades from the 1950s, I saw second stories and cornices from 1888 or 1906.

I learned to spot a "captain's house." These captains, usually Cornishmen, supervised the mining crews. Their homes reflect comfort and prestige. Company houses for miners, enlarged and freshly painted, record a paternalism that met real need yet imposed strict control.

Pompous or modest, in the Keweenaw Peninsula, the older houses crowd close to the street so walkways need less shoveling. Northerly winds sweep moisture from the Big Lake and dump it, frozen, on the Copper Country. A red column stands tree-high by U. S. 41 to show the record-setting total of 1979-1980: 390.4 inches of snow.

Long, gray-white, ponderous, winter controls this land. "When it's minus 40 and blowing, you stay put," remarks Neil Joki, of Sugar Island. "Usually it's about zero, which is comfortable." I saw, and heard, many proofs of winter's rigor. Parking meters, set as far from the curb as possible, leave space for plowed-back snow. On Drummond Island, Lois Borton told me cheerfully, "We had to shovel out to open the museum on Memorial Day." John Hickner, M.D., of Escanaba, cited cabin fever as a contributing cause of obesity and alcoholism.

Most conclusive were two doors at the hotel in Fayette, "down in the banana belt" on the Garden Peninsula. Here the state has restored an iron-smelting community as a historic park, one I liked immensely. Dick Rollenhagen, assistant park manager, pointed out these doors, closed, at the second-story level. In winter they had opened onto a catwalk that led to the upper stage of a two-story outhouse. Snowdrifts would have buried a simple ground-level privy.

Bulky woodpiles caught my eye from the start. These have become standard since fuel prices soared in the early 1970s. "It used to be," says Ingrid Mattson Bartelli of Marquette, "that you judged a woman by her fruit cellar and a man by his woodpile. Maybe we're getting back to that again." Gardener, naturalist, rock hound, Ingrid taught consumers the skills of buying and gathering food until her retirement. Her husband, Leonard, a retired state policeman, had set serving in the U.P. above promotion. *(Continued on page 104)*

Summer's lavish green yields to September's hues in a stand of white birches a hundred yards inland at Pictured Rocks National Lakeshore. Ground cover here includes large-leaved asters and bunchberry, or Canada dogwood. On the lakeshore trail (below, left), hikers climb a landmark of the Painted Rocks area, Miner's Castle, to watch the sun set over the Big Lake. At Marquette, residents and visitors alike often drive through Presque Isle Park to aptly named Sunset Point (below, right), where a wind-wrenched white pine has outlived many savage gales.

Spokesman for and ranking celebrity of the U.P., John Voelker—jurist, novelist, and angler—reviews fine points of dry-fly casting with his guest Rob Cambray. His quarry: "mermaids," alias brook trout. With "Robert Traver" as his pen name, the judge wrote Anatomy of a Murder—*and books on trout fishing. Yesterday's hardware decorates his fishing camp near Ishpeming (left), where one of countless chipmunks nibbles a morsel near a picnic table.*

"We're some of the fortunate ones," says Ingrid, "that could stay here—and still eat!" Her grandfather came from Denmark to homestead a logged-over 40-acre section. Left a widow with seven youngsters, Ingrid's mother took another stump-filled 40 to farm. The oldest child, at 16, Ingrid spent her days at lessons or chores, but the long summer evenings gave her a few free hours. "My time of day is still the evening, when the thrushes are putting their world to bed." Twilight dulled the lilies and Shasta daisies in her garden as she spoke.

Ingrid's father, she told me, died young. He had worked himself "unmercifully," at varied jobs—often, in winter, in virgin swamp, hauling logs down icy trails to a railroad spur. "Each man had his distinctive bells for his team, brass bells. Lovely, lovely tones. And drivers would call for the empty sleighs to give way: *'tuuurrrnnn out!'* Even now I seem to hear those sounds frozen on that February air."

The Upper Peninsula has many haunting presences. Ghost mountains, for one. "Brockway's the rubble of a grand and vanished

Stretching for miles and rising as high as 350 feet, sand dunes mark the "Log Slide" area of Pictured Rocks National Lakeshore, not far from Grand Marais.

PAGES 106-107: Hardwoods brilliant in autumn contrast with luminous—and dangerous—shallows off Grand Island. The abandoned beacon guided mariners into harbor at Munising from 1868 until 1913.

range," geologist Bill Cambray told me. Or ghost beaches. Long ridges above the Big Lake end in terraces the waves and ice planed out ten thousand years gone.

Ghost towns are a difficult category. Chronicler Roy L. Dodge filled a 300-page book with them. On the paved road to Big Bay I passed a neatly carved sign: "Birch. Pop. 0." Does Homestead qualify? "Pop. 6—½ dozen welcomes." Or Tula, "Pop. 9"? On a mud-slick hillside trail near Victoria, history teacher Bruce Johanson pointed out the site of Frenchtown (named for French-Canadians, of course, and one of many, like Swedetowns or Finntowns). "Three or four cabins," he said. "It didn't take much to make a town in those days. And remember, you wouldn't have seen trees then, just stumps."

At the camp meeting of Ewen's yearly Log Jam-bor-ee, I heard priest Gary Jacobs evoke "the roughness, the toughness of the people who lived here . . . our great-grandfathers killing themselves in the forest for 45 cents a day . . . their wives boiling water for the spring washing—imagine what wool clothes smelled like at the end of the winter!—and then wondering where in God's name they could dry them."

Surely no other region honors its forebears more devotedly, or with more realism, than the Upper Peninsula. I heard old jokes, exceedingly ethnic and equally earthy, and old sorrows still fresh in memory. "These people . . ." mused Howard Meadowcroft of the state parks staff. "Their ancestors broke their backs here and died for homes in this country. *They won't leave.* And if circumstances force them to leave I guarantee you they'll come back!"

The U.P. is reunion country: family reunions, ethnic-group reunions, community reunions. Festivals crowd the brief summer, with the Fourth of July a supreme occasion. "Everybody just *zooms* around all day!" says Isabella Sullivan of quiet Munising. In 1890 about half the residents of the U.P. were foreign-born. Today Old Glory flies daily, at home after home, above the cherished marigolds and petunias.

The sun came out splendidly for Brimley's centennial, which comfortably overlapped an annual powwow for Chippewa neighbors at Bay Mills. "There's a big time in the old town today!" said a lady in an old-timey long skirt. Parade units had arrived early from Sault Ste. Marie, Ontario: Unit 2310, Royal Canadian Army Cadets, with kilted pipers; Newman Navy League Cadets and Wrenettes. "One hour's shore leave," barked an officer. "And don't start any barroom brawls!" The Navy stalwarts hit the village swings and seesaw instead.

Senior citizens sat at ease by the curb. Two dolls sat, alertly propped, in a yard. Drums sounded far down Main Street at 2:30: "Here come the horsies!" "Get back, dear!" The Stars and Stripes, the Maple Leaf, a centennial banner all waved proudly. Bikes escorted the float with the senior and the junior kings and queens. The Brimley band, riding hay bales on a flatbed, belted out the Notre Dame fight song. Incumbent politicos rode in state. A challenger shook hands, eagerly, along the sidewalk. Of all the parade units, two captivated me especially: a tepee on a sea of tinsel, with two lovely little girls in a tinsel canoe; and, tractor-drawn, the Smallest Big Top on Earth. Among its well-costumed child stars rode the King of Beasts at Brimley, a stoic yellow Labrador in a ferocious mane of auburn yarn.

Sunlight survived for the Bay Mills powwow next day. A tall center pole and four shorter ones framed a brush arbor for the drummers and singers. A ring with a gate opening eastward defined the dance ground. The drumming stirred my own feet when Bucko Teeple and Gloria Parish led the grand entry: "All rise, please. Gentlemen, remove your hats." A lithe man in dark regalia shortened his steps for a small daughter. A young matron, elegant in beadwork, paused now and then to photograph them. A *(Continued on page 111)*   105

Local celebrations fill the brief U.P. summer. Poised for the grand entry at the Bay Mills Chippewa Reservation powwow, Dennis Shananaquet holds his son, Nodin; youngsters almost as small danced with their elders through an August afternoon. In 1982 a joint festival marked the centennial of nearby Brimley. At right, brothers Dan, left, and Doug Brown relax on their float after Brimley's parade; their dog, Dusty, holds his regal pose as lion of the family circus. Above, in the annual Log Jam-bor-ee at Ewen, Fred and Robert Scheer of Hayward, Wisconsin, cut through a beam in less than ten seconds—racing a chain saw and winning.

long-legged, red-haired girl, rapt and intense, leaped past older women holding a sedate pace. Children just past toddling moved as steadily as did a man in an elaborate "backpiece" of gold and turquoise. Supporting himself on a stick, an old man joined an honor song "for all veterans, Indian and non-Indian."

I had never been to a powwow before, and discussed this one with a friend who has attended many. "Often," he said, "you know you're not wanted. This was the friendliest I've ever seen."

Equally friendly are the U.P.'s delightful small museums and exhibits. These range from the relatively formal, as at the Marquette Historical Society, to the wonderfully haphazard. Alger County has an old home; Luce County, a vintage jail; Iron County, both mining and logging collections. The Ontonagon Historical Society has an array of opera fans and a copper still. Across the street, Stubby's Bar Museum offers a stuffed black bear and the outside chance of a Saturday night row, in a spirit of "I'm feelin' good—anybody wanna take me on?"

In the old days, shop owners and barkeeps might set a bear trap behind the counter as a burglar deterrent. At Daggett, Bildo's Bar Museum has a beauty. Also a stuffed coonalope, a posthumous hybrid of raccoon and pronghorn; antique bottles and new ones, with beer or soft drinks cold at the bar. There you might meet folks who've fled the urban scene down at Menominee (population 10,000).

That city, with an appealing waterfront but no funds at the moment to finish restoring it, has an eloquent marine memorial. The schooner *Alvin Clark*, lost in Green Bay in 1864 and raised in 1969, stands in a timber cradle near the river. A modest shed nearby holds such relics as the captain's greatcoat, torn at the shoulder.

Shipwrecks still underwater attract more and more divers to the northern shore today, and I came to marvel at the missionaries and the voyageurs who traveled these stormy waters from St. Ignace to L'Anse via Sault Ste. Marie.

At the Soo Canals, the world-famous locks orchestrate a deliberate, massive pageant of working ships. The museum ship *Valley Camp*, moored just down channel, lets visitors examine a laker in detail. Displayed on a hatch cover is evidence of the most poignant recent tragedy of the Lakes: the rumpled No. 2 lifeboat of the *Edmund Fitzgerald*, sunk with all hands in the epic storm of November 10, 1975.

"Lake Superior doesn't tune in to the 6 a.m. forecast," I was told. Once I was caught in a thundersquall that made my car tremble like a canoe. Fog, a sustained whiteout, broke my date with Isle Royale, but didn't keep me off the ferry from St. Ignace to Mackinac Island. "Our ferries ran even in the *Fitzgerald* storm," a captain's wife told me. Foghorns called from the mist; fife music rang from the island's fort; horseshoes clipclopped along. Mackinac's horses pull drayloads of hay or carriageloads of day visitors, locally called fudgies because they buy so many pounds of the rival "original" brands of candy. Here the Grand Hotel, which claims the longest porch in the world, lies along a

Skillful "wheelies" divert a schoolboy on a quiet street in Dollar Bay. At Copper Harbor, George Nousiainen (right), a schoolteacher for 25 years, brightens retirement days with business, socializing, and his cherished violin.

ridge side like a stranded luxury liner. This is the last, and most lavish, of Michigan's old summer resorts. I dressed for dinner, in time for the tea-or-champagne hour. "The Grand's *the* exception to a U.P. rule," a friend had advised me. "Elsewhere you might dress up for an occasion, but not just for a restaurant."

Shelter in the U.P. ranges from the Grand's pampering suites, large enough for a quadrille, to uninhabited islands where rocks press through sleeping bags. One night I curled peacefully on soft loam and pine needles, and one motel begged me not to clean fish in my room.

Fishing draws thousands of visitors yearly. Just by showing up I can usually keep fish from biting, but I admired successful dry-fly casting by purists at a truly secret spot, the camp of the U.P.'s distinguished author John Voelker. As "Robert Traver," John wrote a best-seller in *Anatomy of a Murder.* He later resigned his seat on Michigan's Supreme Court to devote himself to the outdoors, brook trout in particular.

John drove me out from Marquette, interpreting the landscape as we crossed high ground rich in hardwoods. "We have our ski areas because glaciers left this tumult of hills and valleys. . . . Now we're on a plateau; the pine loves this sand." A hawk soared over the jack-pine scrub when we stopped to hunt mushrooms. Small apricot-tinted chanterelles had come up in silver-white reindeer moss, between blueberry thickets six inches high. "The bears here are *frantic* because the blueberry crop is bad this year. And the sugarplums are scarce."

John's weathered cabin stands on a private road, "almost as close to Hudson Bay as to Detroit." For guests, he fills glass jars with wild flowers—goldenrod or tansy, bergamot or pinkish lavender star thistle. "When I'm cutting thistle I feel I should kneel and pray." Near the cabin, old church pews, weathered to silver gray, are arranged on rose-gray, ice-scarred bedrock, a "three-and-a-half-billion-year-old carpet." Tag alders line the squelchy margins of John's stream. Tamaracks stand reflected in its pools.

A man of wit, John calls himself "a dismounted John Wayne" and, in fly casting, "a frustrated ballet dancer." He warned a young guest to use less line and an older one to use more, and he sent his own line flicking out as proof that "it's a delicate thing."

John's crony Lloyd Anderson, long retired from his filling station, tied a jewel of a fly for me as he and John told Cousin Jack stories—Cornishmen were Cousin Jacks because they always had relatives they would hire for mining jobs. One story concerned the U.P.'s "national dish," the Cornish pasty, a crusty packet of diced meat and root vegetables: " 'arry says to Sara, 'Lover girl, why don't thee put more mayt in me pasties, me stummick hain't no blawdy root 'ouse!' "

A fisherman younger than John but equally devoted is Greg Mattson of Newberry. Greg knows local waters from tiny creeks to the shores of the Big Lake, and doesn't mind sharing good spots with strangers. At the Upper Falls of the Tahquamenon, a massive cascade of tannin-darkened water, he pointed downstream to an excellent spot for walleye. He called my attention to virgin-stand hemlocks, rare in this logged-over region, to the tiny waterstriders that walleye and perch feed on. In a chain of rapids, the Lower Falls rushes past a small, idyllic island. We rowed out to it and strolled around. "Every little point is a different aspect," Greg said happily. And each offers a different music: whispers on a tiny spillway, treble notes in the shallows, deeper tones where dark torrents leap the boulders. At one vista of amber and diamond sparkles we just stood, watching.

"And people ask me"—Greg's voice sharpened into scorn—" 'Whaddya see up here? There's no jobs, no nothin'.' " He sees the nestling eagles above; the fragment of shell from a freshwater mollusk, "otter and mink food," in the pebbles.

"There's not too many places where you can go a quarter-mile from home and get your bass, or get your deer within a mile. I wouldn't move for all the money in the world. I'll never give up on Newberry—I love it too much." But in 1982 his high-school class couldn't manage a five-year reunion. While their elders return for retirement in small towns and aloof wilderness, the young go away. Yooper graduates scatter, to the colleges, the armed services, the Texas oil rigs, the Wyoming boomtowns.

Greg's friend Charlie Chamberlain, whose great-grandparents settled in Newberry, loves the town too, but it can't give the life he wants. "There's nothing cultural. It's the *ultimate* of rural. I blame the forefathers," he says. "They didn't want factories, or new businesses—new competition. So now the kids bail out, that's why the town's dying."

"Our chief export," a teacher at Iron River said grimly, "is *brains!*"

"The glacier was last night," says John Voelker, whose concern for the Upper Peninsula embraces each aspect of life, "and what is tomorrow?" I looked for the answer he did not offer. I admired U.P. manufactures at the region's first industrial fair, in Marquette. I met public officials and private consultants, financiers and small businessmen, who devote themselves to plans for development. Their successes are real, small in scale, hard won.

However frosty the statistics, life keeps its savor. I met the Marinettes, who lived the French-Canadian saga of logging from the years of the double-bitted ax. The Saykllys of Escanaba, Lebanese by heritage, at the little factory where they made delectable candy. Tony Izzo of Iron Mountain, who's teaching his great-grandson Marcus Anthony the craft of the shoemaker's bench. I sat in a small filling station at Copper Harbor, where George Nousiainen played Finnish songs for me on his 200-year-old violin. "They shift from a major to a minor key," he explained—always sadness, but always a lilt.

One August evening, my friend Dixie Franklin remarked: "I watch the tourists leave at the end of summer. And I think, 'They have to go. And I—I get to stay!' "

The woodlands flared into color. The hunters went out with their dogs. The wind and frost grew sharper. And I, too, had to go, back to the flurry and glitter of urban life.

Lake Superior's spray hangs frozen on bare branches by Keweenaw Bay. Comments one resident, "I've seen ice like that a good quarter-mile inland."

FOLLOWING PAGES: Pleasure craft wait for sunlight and fair wind at Mackinac Island, where summer fog lends the celebrated old resort community the mood of more remote places throughout the Upper Peninsula—an uncrowded peace.

A Blend

# of Sea and Shore
The Gulf Coast

By GENE S. STUART

Photographs by DAN DRY

Pounding hooves beat a staccato cadence as cowboy Dell Smith gallops his quarter horse on South Padre Island, Texas. A barrier island— a strip of land sheltering the mainland from the sea—Padre reveals one facet of the Gulf Coast. Together with other distinctive physical features, including swamps, marshes, deltas, and estuaries, such sandy isles help define a coastal realm that sparkles with variety.

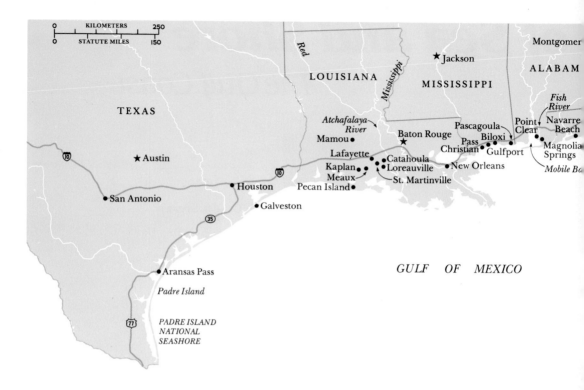

The last surfer had come from the autumn sea, hunched forward and running toward the dunes, hugging the warmth of his chest like a fragile treasure. Wave after rhythmic wave pulsed against the shore. Now, but for drifting gulls and darting sandpipers, I walked the Padre Island beach alone. Here on a windswept stretch of sand I was beginning a trip of some 1,500 miles, one that would take me along the U. S. Gulf Coast from this Texas island to the Everglades of Florida. This living blend of sea and shore—this dynamic, slender world that is the Gulf Coast—has long been a setting for human drama; a pageant of pirates and priests, eccentrics and entrepreneurs, smugglers and settlers. Some have defied it, some have embraced it, but none have ignored this meeting of land and sea.

On Padre Island, mine was a journey through history. As I walked the beach, I passed centuries of submerged shipwrecks, pausing now and then for a respectful moment of sadness, a long gaze for un- known, uncharted disasters. I was on a pilgrimage along the stations of tragedy down this long, lonely shore.

The earliest known disaster happened here in 1554. A Spanish treasure fleet out of Vera Cruz, Mexico, met a tropical storm south of Florida. The storm hurled most of the ships back across the Gulf. Three of the hapless craft sank in Padre Island's shallows, carrying down with them a fortune plundered from the Aztecs. Some 300 men, women, and children struggled ashore from the ships. Most set out overland for the safety of Mexico. Only a few survived the wilderness trek and the Indian attacks along the way. One man, left behind and later rescued, led Spaniards to the wrecks, and divers reclaimed the sil- ver and gold of a conquered empire from the ocean floor.

Curving sweep of shoreline links the two most southerly points in the continental United States, the tips of Texas and of Florida; both lie within 200 miles of the tropics. The arc of the Gulf Coast measures some 1,500 miles. Many of the place-names here echo the original Indian inhabitants. Others recall the Europeans who first came to this region—the Spanish, the French, and the English. Tales of early explorers, adventurers, and settlers add to the colorful legacy of a region still blessed with an array of places off the beaten path.

I knew I could not complete my pilgrimage. It would stretch 113 miles—the length of Padre. In late afternoon I retraced my steps. Hulking oil rigs on the horizon resembled ships riding at anchor to take modern treasure—black gold—from beneath the sea.

At sunset the sky glowed red, a sailor's portent of good weather. Storms, the bane of those who ply the sea, are the most destructive natural force on the Gulf Coast. On the average, two violent storms strike Texas every three years—many with hurricane strength. Only months after my visit, Hurricane Alicia battered the coast, in August 1983.

The most disastrous hurricane and tidal wave in U. S. history struck Galveston, Texas, on September 8, 1900. The tidal surge reached a height of about 20 feet, killing some 6,000 people. One witness reported "roofs of houses and timbers were flying through the streets as though they were paper. . . ." Victims clung to drifting debris throughout the night, and dawn revealed a horrible sight. The tidal wave had swept nearly half the houses in Galveston out to sea.

All have not cowered in the face of violent storms. Pirate Jean Lafitte, larger than life in legend, claimed to have sailed a towering wave across Padre Island in a hurricane just to see if it could be done. Lafitte and other pirates raided the Gulf for riches, and tales of hidden plunder abound. "If Lafitte buried all the treasure that has been claimed," chuckled burly, bearded Richard Harris, a ranger at Padre Island National Seashore, "there wouldn't be any gold left in the world."

Padre Island was the first of many places I visited along the Gulf whose past has been marked by the struggle of individualists against nature. A Portuguese priest, Padre Nicolas Balli, started a ranching tradition in 1800, and the island was named *(Continued on page 124)*

Padre Island lures beachgoers with its many idyllic spots, such as this secluded beach on South Padre. Though millions visit Padre each year, especially the 80-mile stretch of undeveloped land inside the Padre Island National Seashore, the island's wildness still evokes distant days when pirate ships sailed offshore. Today other vessels cruise its waters; at right, Eric Rasmussen wind-surfs off North Padre Island.

Seaside tableau: Shoes rest alongside a collection of shells gathered on a broad Padre Island beach. Longest barrier island in the United States, Padre traces the southern coast of Texas for 113 miles.

Autumnal hues cast an aura of melancholy over the Longfellow-Evangeline State Commemorative Area at St. Martinville, Louisiana. Here a stream glossed with cypress blossoms and leaves meanders past an abandoned cabin. Acadians —French farmers driven from Nova Scotia by the British—first settled in this area near the Bayou Teche in 1765. Longfellow's poem **Evangeline** *recounts their tragic exile; the park, created to memorialize their exodus and relocation, now honors the history of all French in colonial Louisiana.*

for him. In 1884 a high-humored Irishman, Pat Dunn, began raising cattle here. The Duke of Padre, as he called himself, salvaged material from the beach to build an architectural wonder of a two-story house. He found mahogany and pine timbers for the construction. Doors swung on hinges from refrigerators of wrecked steamers. He fashioned doorsteps of coral. The Duke was asked why he made the house so tall. "If I'd had a saw I'd a built a one-story house," his grace is said to have answered. Unfortunately, a hurricane swept the marvel away.

As the age of automobiles arrived, a tourism speculator built a three-mile-long causeway from the mainland to Padre, a raised structure of parallel troughs designed to accommodate, but not necessarily contain, the wheels of a Model T. Fortunately for fainthearted tourists, a hurricane destroyed it as well. But tourism survived, and both ends of Padre became resorts. Most of the land, however, has reverted to the natural barrier island the Spanish shipwreck victims saw. The National Park Service today administers 141,000 acres as Padre Island National Seashore, an 80.5-mile-long park.

"Padre Island is one Texas superlative that is actually true," Rich Harris told me. "It's the longest barrier island in the United States." Repeatedly as I traveled along the Gulf Coast, I found myself in the midst of just such natural superlatives.

An earthen levee in Louisiana separates the farm of Greg Guirard's Cajun boyhood from the Atchafalaya Basin, a wilderness of nearly a million acres that cradles the world's largest cypress and tupelo swamp. Greg has come home after years of study and teaching in other parts of the country, in other parts of the world. At dawn we crossed the levee, near Catahoula, and lowered Greg's boat into the dark water. We entered the swamp and watched a watery world close around us. It is a world of tranquillity or terror by nature's command.

Flocks of small birds, black against the gray sky, chattered in alarm at our approach. Herons and egrets rose from treetops to cross silently to a safer haven. Cypress trunks reflected in still water like heavy skirt folds touching a polished floor. Small trees rained bright yellow leaves upon the dark water. A beaver lodge curved above the surface. Silvery mullet jumped from the water to shatter the liquid mirror with their splashing return.

Occasionally we passed fishermen in other boats. Sometimes we stopped, exchanged greetings, inquired of luck as swampers are inclined to do. Ivory Pete Domingue of Lafayette, fishing for sport, cast his line in an arc. The hook found its mark near a weathered cypress stump. "I picked up 60 bream in half an hour last Thursday," he called. Greg's neighbor, commercial fisherman Roy Blanchard, baited catfish boxes with cheese. "I catch better when the water's low, low like this. I can catch a hundred pounds at a time. That's $50 right there."

Greg, brawny, gentle, and given to introspection, spends several days each week observing and photographing in the swamp. "When I was a boy my grandfather took me deer hunting in here," he recalled. "We'd go with a group of men and sleep on my grandfather's boat or in a camp on top of an Indian mound. Being there, not the killing of deer, was the important thing. To cook and talk and listen to the dogs. The absence of the civilized world, men together in the woods—that's why my grandfather took me. The beauty of it, the wildlife. To me it's a place where people can be separated from society and become more themselves. That's a rare thing."

Such love of place is bred into Cajuns as surely as their love of family, their Catholic faith, and their *joie de vivre*. The French ancestors of the Cajuns traveled a trail of sadness from Acadia, now Nova Scotia, when England deported disloyal French from Canada around 1755. Many Acadians made their way to Louisiana. Longfellow's poem *Evangeline* records their tragic exile; southwestern Louisiana became their home, and through the years, Cadien, then Cajun, their name.

With time the Acadians gathered others into Cajunism. *"Laissez le bon temps rouler"*—let the good times roll—may well be the shout of someone with an English, Scottish, or German surname. For generations the Cajuns remained isolated, surrounded by Anglo-Saxon Protestants who viewed their exuberant lives with stern Calvinistic disapproval, and more than a little silent envy. Acadians brought their language, religion, and customs with them from Canada, but their new land shaped their lives. Those northern farmers adjusted to swamp, bayou, prairie, and marsh—to farm again, fish, hunt, and trap. Activities changed with seasons in lives of joyous independence.

Eddie Boudreaux of Charenton harbors the old ways. He builds boats, fishes, knits nets, grows vegetables, and tends his plant nursery. Cajun French gives music to his voice, and his English flows with an expressive lilt. His eyes sparkled as he spoke. "Oooo, what you talk about. I've done everything. I killed 14 deer in the basin. Hunted duck, squirrel. I trapped. Had a job on a big boat. I'm 78 years old. I like my way of living. I wouldn't want to change. I've got my boats, my fishing; my vegetables produce me good. There's always something to do."

Beyond the swamp to the west, Acadiana, or Cajun country, gives onto prairie. Roads angle sharply to skirt fields planted in soybeans, rice, or sugarcane. November means cane harvest, the burning of the fields. Smoke stung my eyes and filled the air with the odor of burnt sugar. Rice harvest was finished, and clouds of blackbirds swooped to glean stubbled fields. I stopped to watch flocks swirl down, then curve up again like dark ribbons in the wind.

Four straight roads running across the prairie meet at Meaux, a town that even a swamp dweller would call tiny. I stopped there at Maxie Hebert's general store, a weathered and comfortably settled wooden building of some 80 years. Friends had told me that Maxie has sold the store and retired three times, only to buy it back again. Inside, general merchandise occupies one side of the store, a bar stretches along the other, and Maxie's house spans the back portion. When a sprawling modern mall opened in nearby Lafayette, Maxie reacted with wry Cajun humor. He renamed his store and ordered T-shirts emblazoned "Meaux Mall, the Smallest Mall of All."

Not ten minutes after I met the bespectacled, animated Maxie I joined him and three friends in a game of bourré, a favorite Cajun

Pungent smoke from burning sugarcane stings the eyes of farmer Russell Alberts of Coteau Holmes, Louisiana. During the harvest, flames strip cane of foliage, leaving only juice-filled stalks for transport to nearby mills.

pastime akin to poker. We sat at a table at the back of the store. Hand after hand fell to my cards. Maxie ladled homemade soup from the kitchen for the hungry, fetched beer from the bar for the thirsty, performed magic tricks when he grew restless. As the afternoon lengthened, the men praised my unpracticed skills at bourré. Maxie's son returned from a hunt clutching a plastic trash bag full of blackbirds. "Blackbird gumbo tomorrow for Thanksgiving," someone said.

Before I left I asked to buy a T-shirt. Maxie studied his cards with a hooded look. "Ran out and didn't reorder," he muttered. "I'm selling this place in January."

Thanksgiving dawned cold and gray. "We live at the end of the road," Jeb Guidry had told me. That morning we met in Kaplan and drove to Jeb's home. I could see what he meant. "That line of trees," Jeb pointed out. "The earth drops off beyond them. That's where the marsh begins." Tucked into that hidden corner sat Jeb's house and the farm of his in-laws, and I joined them for dinner.

"Thanksgiving? It's not a big holiday with Cajuns," many people had told me. "We celebrate each harvest with a festival—sugarcane, rice, yams, shrimp, crawfish—there are lots of celebrations. Thanksgiving is just another excuse for a family feast."

Outside, Jeb's mother-in-law, Marie Dartez, tended the fire beneath a black caldron. When the oil heated to her satisfaction she tossed in a turkey and two ducks. "Pot-roasted style," she explained. Inside, she served Cajun coffee, pot-black and thick enough to chew, as her husband, Walton, and I settled into rocking chairs in the large kitchen. I told him of my luck at bourré. In spite of his limited English he smiled knowingly. "You play for money?" he asked. "Well, no."

"You play for money, you don't win at bourré," he chuckled.

Throughout the morning the others arrived—21 in all. "Only our son, Michael, is missing," explained Anna Guidry. "He works seven-and-seven on an offshore oil rig. Seven days on the rig, then seven at home. It's our first Thanksgiving without him."

Each arrival prompted the reenactment of a ritual. The newly arrived formed a moving circle inside the circle of the seated, murmuring greetings, kissing. Excitement reached fever pitch with the arrival of the Dartez's seven-month-old great-grandson, Marcus Stelly. By my calculations, kissers and kissees exchanged somewhere near 440 ceremonial smacks. Marcus witnessed all in round-eyed wonder.

The men talked and rocked. The women talked and cooked. When Tammy Hebert burned her finger, Mrs. Dartez grasped it and stood still and silent. "My grandmother's a *traiteur*," said Tammy after a moment. "Her specialty is treating burns. The pain is gone."

"I touch the burn, say a prayer," Mrs. Dartez explained. I had talked to other traiteurs who knew the secret to cure arthritis or sprained ankles or to stop the flow of blood. All agreed the patient must believe in the treatment, must ask *(Continued on page 133)*

Bridal veil bounty: Cajun newlyweds Linda and Mitch Soileau embrace at their wedding reception in Mamou, Louisiana. Following a Cajun custom, male guests have pinned money to the bride's veil for the honor of a dance.

Cajuns of all ages take delight in the cornucopia that is Acadiana. Eddie Boudreaux (above) hauls in a hoop net from the Bayou Teche, adding to the catch already aboard the old-fashioned bateau, which Boudreaux handcrafted. Young celebrators Sandra and Joel Wallins (opposite, top) dance a lively two-step at the Heritage Festival in Loreauville, on the banks of the Teche. At left, a pirogue—a canoe-like Cajun boat—forms a backdrop to a feast of crawfish. Cajuns liken their own proud story of endurance to the legendary bravery of the crawfish.

Songs of sadness, songs of joy: Music from the five-string fiddle of composer-singer Len Harrington of Lafayette, Louisiana, reflects the history of the Cajuns. Harrington's traditional style preserves plaintive ballads sung to fiddles in the 1800s as well as sprightly waltzes and two-steps danced to fiddles and accordions from the turn of the century. Schooled in classical music, Harrington now plays in a Cajun band, preferring the ways of his folk-musician father and grandmother. He hears in the music "a sadness, reflecting hard work and suffering, but also high spirits and humor. The music is the heart and soul of Cajun people—a unifying factor in a dying culture."

to be cured. And the traiteur must not accept pay in return. Cajun traditions have deep roots, often older than Acadiana itself.

When the birds cooking outside had bubbled to a burnished gold, the dining table was laid for the men to sit down together and begin the feast. The women served them: turkey, duck, rice dressing, vegetables—dishes by the score. Only afterward did they see to the children and themselves at other tables, a mealtime priority observed by French farm folk hundreds of years ago and kept alive by rural Cajuns today.

While the Dartez family nurtures tradition and that rich quality of life that is Cajunism, it also demonstrates change in Acadiana. Until recent years, trapping, hunting, and fishing typified Cajun life. Today it is just as common to meet a Cajun college professor, bank president, or oil millionaire. Many of Mr. and Mrs. Dartez's generation grew up speaking only Cajun French and attending school sporadically at best. They had little need for literacy. By contrast, Jeb Guidry is bilingual, and as principal of Kaplan High School supervises the education of a maturing generation. Young Marcus may never learn Cajun French.

"My grandmother didn't speak English," composer-musician Len Harrington told me. "She used to refer to *les américains*. I was in high school before I realized the words meant 'Americans,' not 'those people who speak English.' My wife does not speak French. I've taught my son a few words, but he doesn't really hear it at home. Mine is one of the last generations to grow up in both languages."

Artist Gerard Sellers forgot the Cajun French of his childhood. He left the marsh three times, but he always returned. The last time, he stayed. Gerard is a bear of a man, as big-bearded as he is shiningbald, with dark eyes that could stop an autumn wind with a glance. As we shared a meal of fried alligator in Abbeville, he recalled, "I relearned the language, found family and security again, warmth and friendliness, and customs that make you feel welcome, like a hand fitting into a comfortable glove."

Gerard now works seasonally as a hunting guide and is one of several Cajuns who collect local folklore and oral history. He explained, "When I was living in Houston it struck me that people there had just put men on the moon; two hours' drive away my people were still skinning alligators. Our way of life is rapidly disappearing. If we can get young people to talk to their parents and grandparents, record it now, and take pride in it, in 40 years it will still be alive." Gerard concluded, "I think of myself as a young Cajun bridging the gap between tradition and technology to build a future."

*E*ast of Louisiana's marshy coast, beyond the great delta the Mississippi has thrust into the Gulf, sandy beaches appear again. The world's longest and widest man-made beach stretches up to 300 yards in width and some 26 miles in length in the area of Gulfport and Biloxi, Mississippi. Long before the beach was built, people summered here. They came to enjoy cool breezes or to escape the dreaded miasmas, vile

Duck decoys bobbing, Cliff DeLouche and his son, John, take aim in a salt marsh near Pecan Island. Louisiana's "trembling prairies" once yielded a year-round harvest of waterfowl for Cajuns. Hunting now attracts sportsmen seasonally.

exhalations of the earth they believed brought epidemics of yellow fever and other diseases. Most of the old houses fronting the shore are gone now. The few that remain serve as shrines to a sometimes sentimentalized, sometimes violent past. Massive oaks, magnolias, and cedars shade Bouvoir, the last home of Jefferson Davis. The aging President of the Confederacy came here after Civil War defeat, "a citizen of no land under the sun, proscribed, misrepresented, and derided." He spent his final years here writing his Confederate history, taking solitary walks, and sitting alone beside a peaceful spring.

Today the house is a museum, and more. The presence of its occupants lingers still, in a setting quiet enough to sense a heartbeat. A serene sadness overlies imposing furniture, family portraits, flowers pressed as treasured memories. Tradition says a beloved daughter, Winnie, died of heartbreak for a forbidden Northern lover.

I gazed for a time from a window. Panes of old, wavy glass distorted the view. Immobile tree trunks seemed to sway, a rose garden was magnified to a riotous forest, familiar shapes rippled and angled. It was as if I saw reality as an unreal dream through eyes from the past.

It is reported that camels hauled cypress logs from swamps for Bouvoir's construction. It is known that slaves built it. The slave trade made the builders of Longfellow House, near Pascagoula, Mississippi, wealthy. The house remains one of the most majestic along the Gulf Coast; the history of its builders, one of the most horrible. Mrs. Carlen Graham beat her slaves unmercifully, bound them in chains. Some did not survive her treatment.

White columns front the grand facade of Longfellow House. Curving stairways sweep toward the sea. It is said that Longfellow paid a visit and while here wrote a poem of building ships. The house took his name. Some believe ghosts haunt the now unoccupied mansion.

One morning, as sunlight alternated with gloomy rain, I wandered through the first floor, past a workman busy at restoration, past black marble mantels veined with beige, beneath bell-shaped chandeliers. In sunlight, tear-shaped prisms echoed crystal raindrops on the windowpanes. Alone, I slowly mounted the curving stairway to the upper floor, where bloodstains in the hall attest some forgotten tragedy. At the top of the stairs a closed door in the hallway seemed foreboding, threatening. I paused, not sure I wanted to continue. Suddenly, a beam of sunlight struck the silvery doorknob, giving it an eerie glow. Though no ghost, I could have sworn I proved it possible to pass through solid walls, emerging on the front lawn in a matter of seconds.

The thrust of Clifford James's jaw defies fear. "I'm a blue-eyed Cherokee on my momma's side," said Jamie. "Daddy claimed he was half rattlesnake and half barbwire fence."

I jutted my jaw to ride with him on one of the last United States postal routes delivered entirely by boat. In Magnolia Springs, Alabama, near Mobile Bay, we climbed into a 16-foot fiberglass craft for the 25-mile run down the Magnolia River, across Weeks Bay, up the Fish River and back again—123 mailbox stops. There were small-craft warnings that morning, with seas running four to six feet. "Wind's gusting up to 40 miles an hour," Jamie grinned, elated by the challenge. "I was in the Navy 27 years. I first heard the song of the sea on an aircraft carrier in the '50s. Once you hear it, it never leaves your ears."

We motored down the ice-cold, spring-fed Magnolia, across the blackness of a spot called Devil's Hole. "They know it's at least 300 feet deep, but they haven't found bottom yet." Jamie stood spraddle-legged to run the boat with one hand and stuff mailboxes perched over the water with the other. He approached each box in a different way, drifting alongside, angling crabwise, or butting head-on against a pier

Welcoming glow from Belvedere, a mansion in Pass Christian, Mississippi, evokes southern hospitality of long tradition. Beginning before the Civil War, wealthy families built homes here, many since destroyed by fire or storm.

to bounce back into his route. As we slapped across the corrugated surface of Weeks Bay, running with the wind and tide, Jamie shouted above the storm, "I've had six-foot waves break my glasses. I've been knocked unconscious three times in 45 minutes trying to get into this bay. One woman told me I ought to carry an umbrella. I said, 'Just as soon as I grow a tail to hold it.' I delivered mail in Hurricane Frederic and didn't run late. Couldn't go the next day, though, the water was too full of trees and furniture."

We eased up the calm Fish River, up quiet sloughs, past tunnels in tall grass that led to alligator nests. "I've had six alligators at a time come running from the bank," said Jamie. "Just like a Tarzan movie."

We donned slickers for the run back across Weeks Bay. Jamie secured a rope to a railing for me to grasp and we sped into a blinding spray, crashing from the top of one whitecap to the next, running against the wind. Stormy Mobile Bay churned beyond us. I could not loosen my grip to wipe water from my eyes. I dared not talk for fear of drowning in my own words. Ten minutes in a tempest seems a lifetime.

And suddenly we were once again on the peaceful Magnolia. This time I was delighted to cross Devil's Hole. "The rivers and bays—each has a different sound," I said. Jamie shot me a knowing look. "The song of the sea," he commented. As we moored the boat, Jamie said almost as an afterthought, "Today was about the same as Hurricane Frederic." I felt saturated with gratitude that he hadn't told me earlier.

Along the Eastern Shore of Mobile Bay, a unique phenomenon happens without warning—a gift on an incoming tide. In mild weather, with a gentle wind blowing from the east, the water assumes a brownish cast, and eels rise to the surface. Area natives read the signs with the gusto of a gourmand perusing a classic menu. The cry of "Jubilee" is passed up and down the shore, and residents rush out with tubs, nets, baskets, and whatever else will hold a bounty of seafood. Masses of crabs or shrimps or flounder—sometimes a mix of fish and shellfish—have gathered in the shallows and remain there for the taking. Some experts explain Jubilees as a sudden drop in aquatic oxygen supply, causing a kind of stupor in the sea life.

"We don't have a Jubilee every year," Ruthie Henning of Point Clear told me. "Then again, it might happen two or three times in one week. Once, my aunt, a nun, was visiting. The shouting started and she jumped out of bed, grabbed a gig, and ran out without her habit.

Alabama mailman Clifford James makes his rounds along Mobile Bay's Eastern Shore on one of the few remaining U. S. postal routes covered entirely by boat. James uses alternate land routes only to avoid floods or hurricane debris.

When the sun came up she was still standing in the bay in her nightgown and sleeping cap, happily gigging flounder."

A seashore bounty of another kind spreads along some of Florida's sandy barrier isles. On Captiva and Sanibel Islands, the Gulf's powerful tides and currents strew shells by the waveful onto the beach, and visitors by the thousand find in them a treasure.

The islands are at once a haven for shell collectors and a home to wildlife. In Sanibel's J. N. "Ding" Darling Wildlife Refuge, I felt an intruder in nature's realm when an anhinga, perched in a mangrove tree, eyed me with coy vulnerability and spread its storm-dark wings to dry after a morning of underwater fishing. At a nearby lagoon, I watched an alligator, as motionless as a bumpy log, lie in wait while mottled ducks just out of snapping range calmly ignored the predator.

Tradition says pirates found sanctuary on Captiva and Sanibel. According to one legend, the notorious Spaniard Gasparilla made Captiva a prison for captive women, a legacy that gave the island its name. A man who claimed to have been a member of Gasparilla's crew, Juan Gomez, was said to have become a hermit on Panther Key in the Ten Thousand Islands, which fringe the Everglades. He died in 1900 claiming to be 122, ending his days in a house built of driftwood and the wreckage of ships, mumbling mysteriously of jewels, doubloons, and pieces of eight.

Solitude is a hermit's sublime desire, and I have found no better place for solitude than in the Ten Thousand Islands. Here I again roamed superlatives. In the Everglades, a vast sea of grass unique in the world, a river six inches deep and 50 miles wide forever slides toward the sea; where fresh and salt water meet, the Ten Thousand Islands form the nation's only mangrove forest.

I explored that primeval wilderness by boat with National Park Service ranger Robert Gibbs, tall, tanned, and an expert in forestry. We wandered the complex of islands, through narrow passageways, up wide rivers. Pirates of another kind now haunt the islands: Drug smugglers, usually under the cover of darkness, make landfalls in hidden byways. Bob and I stopped to explore the highest point in the Everglades, an Indian shell mound 20 feet tall.

Everywhere, decaying mangrove leaves transformed the water into a black tea. The nutritious brew feeds small organisms at the bottom of the food chain in this nursery of nature. Each twisting turn in the maze of islands became a revelation of wildlife: herons, egrets, and white ibis gliding on the wind; cormorants bobbing up from beneath the surface; kestrels watchful from lofty treetop nests.

Often we passed small solitary mangroves, the nuclei of new islands that would form from sand, silt, and debris trapped in their tangled roots. To Bob, each island is a landmark. I no longer had a sense of direction, but it was of no concern. Bob commented, "Sometimes when I'm out here and hear a kestrel's cry or see a flock of white pelicans in flight, I'm amazed that I'm paid for doing this."

My journey was drawing to an end. I had traveled from the tip of Texas nearly to the tip of Florida. Along the way I had been an adventurer, an observer, an intruder, and a welcome guest. I had encountered a grand sweep of history here on the Gulf Coast, from Cajun stories of joy and sadness to tales of buried pirate treasure. As Bob guided our boat homeward now across the dark water, I knew that I possessed a treasure of my own—a trove of lasting memories of this alluring world of land and sea.

FOLLOWING PAGES: *Sunset burnishes a golden path for strollers on Navarre Beach in Florida's panhandle, an area of inviting sugar-white strands.*

Brown pelicans and cormorants sprout from the greenery of a red mangrove tree in Florida's Ten Thousand Islands. The waters of the Gulf support a bounty of sea life, attracting water birds to the thousands of mangrove islands here. At left, roots of sea oats and low-lying vines stabilize a fragile dune on Florida's Pavilion Key, one of the few of the Ten Thousand Islands with a sand beach.

FOLLOWING PAGES: Maze-like wilderness of mangrove islands spreads into the sea near the tip of Florida, eastern end of the long arc of the Gulf Coast.

Jewel of the

The Ozarks

By THOMAS O'NEILL

Photographs by MATT BRADLEY

With corn kernels and acorn caps for pieces, Mary Lee Pinkerton, age seven, and Delanna Lacy play the Ozark version of Fox and Geese. Mary and Delanna—both dressed in 19th-century attire—sit at a desk in a one-room log schoolhouse at the Ozark Folk Center. Since its opening a decade ago in Mountain View, Arkansas, the center has sought to keep alive the rich tradition of Ozark folklore, handicrafts, and music.

Heartland

Maybe the moon was full, or perhaps a jug of white lightning was making itself felt. How else explain a fit of bragging that overtook some fellow in the Ozark town of Green Forest, Arkansas? The story—as told by the late folklorist Vance Randolph—goes that the man just got in the mood to holler.

"I'm so tough," the Ozarker proclaimed, "I can scoot down a honey-locust back'ards, with two wildcats in each hand, an' never git a scratch! I got ears like a 'backer-leaf, sides like a wagon-bed, iron ribs an' a steel backbone! I got a wire tail, an' it screwed on! Hi-yoop!"

From the sound of it, a mean scrap-metal Goliath was on the loose in Green Forest. But then again, probably only a hot rusty wind was blowing from a front-porch idler. What the small-town blusterer was saying in his own way was simply that he was like nobody else. Judging from my stay in the region, he could have been speaking for many an Ozarker.

It didn't take more than a few days for me to realize I had stepped into a singular world indeed when I entered the Ozark hill country, the thickly forested uplands region comprising most of southern Missouri and northern Arkansas, the northeastern corner of Oklahoma, and small parts of Kansas and Illinois. I soon learned that the hillbilly character Vance Randolph described some 50 years ago is today found chiefly at amusement parks and craft centers. But I also learned that time-honored customs and folkways continue to be observed throughout the Ozarks, especially in rural areas, where I traveled most.

One Saturday in October, while on a typical twisting and turning drive through countryside aflame with color, I pulled up to a line of pickups—the indispensable Ozark vehicle—stopped alongside the road in Hurley, Missouri. The truck beds were piled high with black walnuts that had been collected from nearby fields and yards and hauled here for sale. The Ozark area is a major producer of black walnuts, and gatherings like this occur all across the region each fall.

A sign announced the going rate: "Seven dollars a hundred pounds." In the background a noisy machine was stripping the thick green hulls off the nuts. As the machine chewed and clattered, I joined the walnut pickers while they waited to unload their harvest. Conversations eddied around such predictable topics as the weather, the price of livestock, and who's doing what in the family. Yet every so often I heard something that made these everyday subjects seem unusual.

"It's going to be a severe winter," a woman informed me. "I split open a persimmon and the seeds were in the outline of a spoon. That means you'll be eating gruel this winter."

"See this hedge apple," another woman said, holding up a large green fruit whose squiggly texture resembled the surface of the human brain. "You put it under your sink, and you'll never have another cockroach."

"Don't tell this to anybody," a large man wearing a farm cap whispered to me. "But I can show you a silver mine on my property. You know, that lost mine the Spaniards were looking for."

As I was walking back to my car, shaking my head in wonder, an owl began to hoot in the woods, even though the sun was shining brightly. "You hear that?" someone said. "That means there'll be a change in the weather soon."

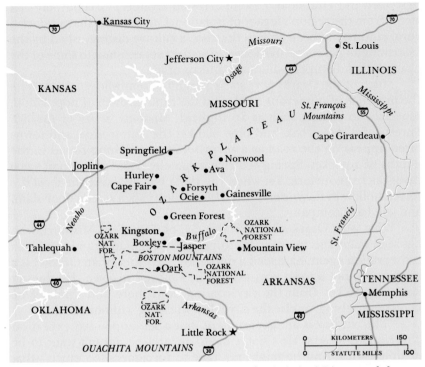

Heartland jewel: Bounded by the Missouri and Mississippi Rivers and the Arkansas River Valley, the scenic Ozarks cover 50,000 square miles of southern Missouri and northern Arkansas, spilling into Oklahoma, Kansas, and Illinois.

I had come to a niche in the country where, for some, superstitions and folklore flow through life as naturally as clouds cross the sky. As the weeks of my visit sped by, I came to see that many aspects of rural Ozark life bore the stamp of individuality—from the old-time music and the zest for the outdoors to bartering and even the interpretation of the law.

Geographically the Ozark region is also distinct. Boundaries abound. The Ice Age glaciers stopped just above the Missouri River, the northern border of the Ozarks. The prairie abuts the region's western edge; the humid Mississippi lowlands begin at its southeastern end; and the Arkansas River Valley forms its southern boundary. The one overlapping feature comes from the east, the Ozarks marking the farthest advance of the great eastern deciduous forest.

Otherwise, the region remains a geographical oasis. Together with the Ouachita Mountains just to the south, the Ozarks exist as the only extensive relief between the Appalachians and the Rocky Mountains. There are no real mountains in the alpine sense. The highest point rises only to 2,561 feet, in northwestern Arkansas. Yet the ridges are numerous enough and tough enough to have isolated parts of the Ozarks until World War I. Military service forced young men out of the hills, and later the tourism industry began to discover the lovely, rugged landscape. Before then, the Ozarks sometimes seemed easier to go around than to travel across. Robert Flanders, director of the Center for Ozarks Studies at Southwest Missouri State University, has described the Ozarks as a "semi-arrested frontier," a condition that stems from the region's legacy of isolation. One result is that a colorful rural culture has been able to flourish, a culture distinguished by the intermingling of successive waves of settlers yet resistant to some of the changes that disrupt traditional patterns of life.

Much of the Ozarks persists as a realm of semiwilderness, despite the presence of numerous roads and the rapid growth of population, especially in centers such as Springfield, Missouri, a city of 133,000. Forests of hickory, oak, and pine blanket the countryside, and towns often appear on the road as a surprise, like something found in the depths of a pocket. Spring-fed rivers run clear, and more than 5,000 caves pock the surface. Yet when you think you've found the most deserted hollow in the county, you'll hear a dog yap, a screen door slam, and you have company.

What is an Ozarker? Bob Walsh, 55, of Cape Fair, Missouri, who has seen many specimens in his sometimes rough-and-tumble job as a conservation agent, hazarded a definition. "My idea of an Ozarker is a hill person, not a town boy, even if he's moved to town. He doesn't want any slicker from the city coming down here and thinking he knows everything, or else the city feller will leave without his hide.

"The old boy is antigovernment, but a self-appointed expert on government affairs. He's not a meddler, and he doesn't want to be meddled with. And he might not take to foreigners too much—that means anyone outside the county." To this flavorful definition I can add a few more items. The rural Ozarkers I met were shrewd and self-reliant, and many were handy with the hands, especially the old-timers. One Ozarker remarked to me, "You take 90-year-old Aunt Ella and seal her off in a holler, and she'll outlive us all."

One of the highest compliments that can be paid an Ozarker is that he or she is a good storyteller. And it is true that Ozarkers are sometimes wary of strangers; stares almost pushed me out of a cafe in one Ozark town. Yet when I was introduced to someone simply as a friend of a friend, all hospitality broke loose.

My favorite description of the Ozark character came from Bob Holt, a dairy farmer from Ava, Missouri. After telling me of a few of his escapades, Bob suddenly said, "People should know—I'm more independent than a hog on ice." I met Bob one day while scouting the countryside of Douglas County with Gordon McCann, a Springfield businessman who in his spare time turns into an amateur folklorist and goes searching for practitioners of traditional Ozark music. Gordon said that Bob was the fastest old-time square dance fiddler he knew.

We pulled up to a small, sturdy farmhouse and were greeted by two dogs that had been asleep in back. Like many rural Ozarkers, Bob, 52, lives within eyeshot of the now ramshackle house where he was born and raised. Once we were inside, it took little encouragement for Bob to lift his fiddle from its case and, with Gordon accompanying him on guitar, run through a few high-spirited (Continued on page 155)

Powered by a spring flowing 24 million gallons a day, the Hodgson Mill produced cornmeal and flour in Ozark County, Missouri, for nearly a hundred years. Though now it stands silent, the mill remains open to visitors.

NATIONAL GEOGRAPHIC PHOTOGRAPHER BRUCE DALE

Young Ozarkers hone hunting skills by taking target practice with pellet guns near Ava, Missouri. Monks from a Trappist monastery built the bridge on which the boys stand. Hunting ranks high among rural Ozark activities. "I believe," observed the author, "a good number of Ozarkers wouldn't mind if heaven turned out to be a vast hunting preserve." At top, men catch up on local news outside the Henson Store near Norwood, Missouri. Above, customers shop for groceries, feed, and gas at the general store that has served the county for half a century.

Eighty-three years of Ozark living etch the face of Clark Lambert, who pauses at his blacksmith shop in Douglas County, Missouri. Lambert began teaching himself his trade at age 16. He also farms, and he has been a minister for 50 years. Both lifelong Ozarkers, Lambert and his wife raised ten children.

tunes with names like "Soppin' the Gravy," "Pig Ankle Rag," and "Rabbit in a Pea Patch." It was impossible to keep our feet still.

After a while, Bob, who figures he knows 300 or so fiddle tunes, wiped his brow and talked about the music. "Ozark-style music has got a distinctive sound, but it's hard to explain," Bob said in a voice so deep it seemed to be coming from the bottom of a barrel. "I've heard enough to know it sounds different from fiddling in central and northern Missouri. It's got more of the individual in it, more feeling. And darn it, it's better dance music; it's better to put your foot down to."

Back in Bob's parents' time and before, fiddling amounted to one of the few forms of entertainment, even though a lot of churchgoing people branded the fiddle as the "devil's box," and refused to allow it in their homes. The fiddle was so prized that youngsters were made to practice it over a feather bed in case they dropped it. Musicians carefully wrapped their fiddles in empty flour sacks to protect them when they rode horses to square dances.

One evening I went to hear Bob Holt play at a square dance. A large machine shed on a farm north of Ava had been converted to a dance floor for Saturday night. Three dozen people were milling around the food table when Bob drew his bow a few times across his fiddle's amplified strings, signaling that the dancing should begin.

"Decorate the floor," Bob cried, launching into a driving tune as two groups of eight people, each with its own caller, hurriedly took their places. Within seconds a din arose, made up of roughly equal parts of stomping feet, clapping hands, and racing fiddle. "Is your arm broke? We just got our wind." Host Jerry Wagner was teasing Bob, who had taken a pause. The music fired up again. A young man named Johnny Reed, who was wearing taps on his heels and toes, got the crowd hollering when he broke into a jig like some lively puppet.

Then the wasps attacked. Before the dance they had gone unnoticed, clustered on one of the overhead beams. They had come indoors to find places for winter nests, and at first were sluggish in the chill air. But as the shed heated up, so did the wasps. With the dancers swirling round the floor, the wasps began swooping down from the ceiling. Every so often a dancer would yell in alarm, leap from the dance floor, wave his arms wildly, then quickly rejoin his partner, hardly missing a step. It was Ozark improvisation at its best.

During my travels I quickly found that Ozarkers love to talk about their region and their way of life. It is incomprehensible to many of them that anyone would want to be shut up in a city. One day I was driving in Arkansas with a sparkling river on one side and sandy bluffs scented with sassafras on the other, when my companion, Billy Higgins, who helps run the country store in Oark, suddenly exclaimed, "Sometimes I can't believe I'm living in such beautiful country. There's clean air, clear water, no congestion." Billy halted a moment and then laughed to himself. "Only thing is, it's hard to make a living."

"We love wood, the feel of it taking shape in your hands," say wood-carvers Gerry and Sheri Phillips-Chisholm. Attracted by rural Ozark life and the friendly people, the couple came to Mountain View, Arkansas, from Tennessee 11 years ago. A quizzical raccoon (right) clutches a fish in one of their carvings.

Prosperity has never come easy to the Ozarks. Except for the river bottoms and upland prairies, the land is steep and rocky, with thin, poor soil. Crop farming is often a toss-up proposition. Most farmers make a living from livestock. The most plentiful resource has always been trees, and in the latter half of the 19th century, the lumber industry boomed, at times almost denuding the countryside. Ozark forests provided many of the ties for the railroad tracks then being laid across the continent. Mounds of sawdust still appear on the sides of country roads, residue of small working sawmills, but the big paydays of the timber boom ceased long ago.

*I*n the eastern Ozarks, lead mining has bolstered the economy since the 1700s, when French explorers searching for minerals found rich deposits of lead. Some believe the word *Ozark* comes from the name of a French trading post on the Arkansas River—*Aux-arcs*. Cavernous mines exist in the vicinity of the St. François Mountains, supplying 90 percent of the lead extracted in the United States. Lead and zinc mining also have been important in the western Ozarks, in the area around Joplin, Missouri.

Ever resourceful, rural Ozarkers have sometimes helped earn a living by trapping raccoon and mink or by digging up ginseng root. Prized in the Orient as an aphrodisiac and for its supposed medicinal qualities, ginseng root, which grows wild in the Ozarks, can fetch its harvesters more than a hundred dollars a pound.

The most recent and most exotic crop to surface in the Ozarks is one that is illegal: marijuana. Introduced in the early '70s and grown on remote hillsides, marijuana has become a lucrative cash crop in Missouri and Arkansas. According to the Drug Enforcement Administration, the two states rank among the top ten in the country in production of the outlaw plant.

Most Ozarkers condemn what they consider to be an unsavory intrusion from the outside world, but marijuana has definitely infiltrated Ozark life. Talking with the sheriff of Newton County, Arkansas, I happened to look up at his wall of shelves. On the top shelf stood the expected lineup of marksmanship trophies and confiscated weapons. On the second shelf: a row of water pipes.

One facet of the Ozark economy I found interesting is the bartering that takes place. County newspapers carry ads in which someone is willing to swap his house for someone else's. Farmers will trade a hog or the use of a tractor for help during the haying season. Once I spotted a 1960 Thunderbird sports coupé in a barn.

"How much you pay for that beauty?" I asked.

" 'Bout five calves," the owner answered.

I never heard of anyone trading a hunting dog. From what I gathered, hard cash changed hands when dogs were bought or sold, often quite a lot of it. A well-pedigreed Walker hound, for instance, can go for as much as $1,500. Anything for that matter associated with hunting—dogs, guns, four-wheel-drive pickups, even hunting buddies—is immensely valuable to many Ozarkers, perceiving of hunting as they do as one of life's inalienable rights and pleasures. I believe that a good number of Ozarkers wouldn't mind if heaven turned out to be a vast hunting preserve with not a game warden in sight.

There are bird dogs and coonhounds, wolfhounds and foxhounds, and to raise the issue of which breed is better suited to a specific mission is to risk lengthy soliloquies and combative arguments. "You can talk about a man's wife before you talk about his dogs," one hunter advised me.

In the Ozarks, men still gather in the dead of a winter night on lonely ridgetop roads, build themselves a fire, and release a pack of swift foxhounds. Soon the hoarse *aarw aarw aarw* of the dogs begins echoing in the fields and woods below. The men then spend the cold night huddled around the fire, taking keen enjoyment in listening to the sounds of the invisible hunt, as if the yelps and howls of the individual dogs made up a superb choral arrangement.

Each man knows the distinctive bark, or mouth, of each dog, and thus is able to visualize the nocturnal chase. "There's your coarse-mouthed Abner leading the pack." "That chop-mouthed Buddy jumped a fox. Listen! They're down by the creek and headin' north." Near daybreak the men return to their homes with the exhausted hounds. Rarely do the dogs catch a fox, but the men don't mind, for their pleasure is the hunt itself.

In the early 1800s, when numbers of settlers began arriving in the

Computer-age "cowpoke," seven-year-old Little Bear Muskrat, a Cherokee Indian, learns to use a terminal at his school near Stilwell, Oklahoma. Although at home in the modern world, descendants of Cherokees driven from the East in the 1830s strive to preserve their cultural heritage in the Oklahoma Ozarks.

interior of the Ozarks—most of them from Tennessee and Kentucky and most of Scotch-Irish descent—hunting often provided the margin of survival. Today the frontier notion of being able to look after oneself in the outdoors, and of revering the forests and streams for all that they offer, remains indispensable to the identity of certain Ozarkers.

Jack Richards professed this attitude the time we floated Beaver Creek in Missouri. It was a 70-degree *(Continued on page 164)*

Jagged sandstone outcropping juts above a deep, wooded valley near the Buffalo River in Newton County, Arkansas. Members of the Ponca Photography Workshop, an annual seminar, photograph the fall color from the natural overlook. The Ozarks once provided a hunting ground for Osage Indians, then forestland and farms for a succession of settlers. Though long exploited by man, the Ozark region remains largely a realm of semiwilderness—a rugged, cave-riddled landscape where hundreds of rivers and streams course among the hills. The creek below cascades down a stairway of moss-covered stone in the Boston Mountains of Arkansas, inside the Ozark National Forest. Below, at right, a maidenhair fern radiates delicate fronds in a moist woodland area of the Boston Mountains.

TIM ERNST (ABOVE AND LEFT)

159

"Our mountains ain't so high," goes one Ozark saying, "but our valleys shore are deep." Tucked into many of those valleys are small farms such as this smoke-wreathed homestead south of Jasper, Arkansas. Below, James Whitaker, in the company of his daughters April, five, and Jamie, eight, hauls water to his house near Mountain View, Arkansas. Whitaker and his wife came to the Ozarks eight years ago in search of an alternative to city life. Say the Whitakers, "The book of experience teaches us every day things that our forefathers took for granted—the right way to plant a fruit tree, how to store foods . . . basically, how to live a self-sufficient life."

Canoeists huddle around a fire as chill morning mists rise from the Buffalo River in the heart of the Arkansas Ozarks. Once threatened by three dams, the Buffalo's meandering waters still flow free—protected within a national park. At left, boys frolic on a sultry summer day in one of the river's deep, clear pools.

day in November, and Jack, whose occupation for much of his 55 years has been that of hunter and fisherman, was demonstrating his skill with a gig. Standing in the stern of the canoe, he would hold the 14-foot pole poised in his hand. At its end were four prongs. Spotting a fish darting through the clear water, Jack would let the pole fly. More often than not he came up with a big chunky fish, locally called a red-horse. The Osage Indians who used the Ozarks as hunting grounds could not have done much better.

Jack, who lost his two front teeth and has never bothered to replace them, doesn't say much to people he doesn't know well. Yet after filling the canoe with fish, he became expansive as we drifted down the peaceful creek. Mentioning a vacation trip he took to Nevada, Jack said, "I wouldn't trade my backyard for all that country around Las Vegas. If I can't see trees or water, I don't like it. This here is the best country a man can have. He has everything to do. I don't like to be crowded, either. I need a lot of freedom, and I have it here."

This idea of freedom can also extend to matters of authority and law enforcement. Many Ozarkers, particularly in remote areas, don't want outside agencies interfering in their affairs. The cartoon image of a hillbilly chasing away a revenuer at gunpoint is not wholly fictitious. I met one man who at age 78 ran a pair of engineers off his property with a rifle when they began surveying for a new sewer line.

Some Ozarkers still adhere to the biblical injunction of an "eye for an eye." During my visit I heard unnerving stories of house burnings, bloody fistfights, and shootings. In most cases the incident was explained away as the settling of some private matter. As Bob Holt of Douglas County said, "When scratched, they bleed violent down here."

Douglas Mahnkey, who has been practicing law in Forsyth, Missouri, since 1935, told me of the highly personal attitude held toward the law by many Ozarkers. "They'll turn you in for murder or rape, but if you're making moonshine, cutting government timber, or hunting deer out of season, they may keep their mouths shut."

Just as rumors of moonshining continue to hang on in rural areas, so do tales of feuding. Though probably all of the old feuds have withered away, memories can still be powerful. Gordon McCann told me that "at the last moment a county dropped the chapter on one feud from its centennial history for fear it would stir things up again."

Strong family loyalties exist throughout the Ozarks. The mere mention of a family name can inspire long discussions of the family tree plus bits of savory gossip. As one person informed me soon after my arrival in the Ozarks, "When you run out of things to talk about, you can always talk about family."

I saw homes in which the living room walls were covered with pictures of relatives. There were people who seemed to know the family names of everyone in their county. Such extensive knowledge of the local clans provides a form of shorthand in the passing of information. Phrases such as "He married a Ferguson girl" or "His mother was a Smith" contain reams of details and nuances for Ozark natives.

Some family names that one might hear in the Ozarks are more surprising—Muskrat, Mankiller, Polecat, Hawk. They belong to Cherokee Indians who live in the northeastern corner of Oklahoma. It was here in the Ozark hills that some 14,000 Cherokees settled 145 years ago, expelled from their homelands in Tennessee, North Carolina, and Georgia by the United States government. Their forced trek westward in the winter of 1838-39 became known as the Trail of Tears.

Since their abrupt resettlement, the Cherokees have become part of the Ozarks culturally as well as geographically. There are Indian fiddlers who play at hoedowns. There are Baptist churches where Cherokees sing hymns on Sunday. In several homes I found Cherokee women piecing beautiful quilts, using traditional, non-Indian designs such as "wedding ring" and "drunkard's path."

Betty Smith is a full-blood Cherokee who manages the Cherokee National Museum near Tahlequah, capital of the old Cherokee Nation, which existed from 1839 to 1907, when it was absorbed by the new state of Oklahoma. Betty told me about superstitions and medicinal remedies that are the same as those recorded half a century ago in Missouri and Arkansas by Vance Randolph. Among the cures Betty remembered her mother using were rubdowns with skunk grease for chest colds, and the application of pork-fat poultices to boils.

Sometimes the overlap of cultures strikes a curious note. One day I went to a remote cabin to meet an old woman who spoke only Cherokee. When I arrived, a seven-year-old boy stood outside staring at me as he chewed a plug of tobacco. Inside, the old woman wouldn't come out of the kitchen, too shy even to look at a white stranger.

While I sat alone in the front room, feeling as if I had crossed into a foreign country, a young Indian woman came out holding a brown-skinned baby on her hip. The infant had jet black eyes and hair, and his high cheekbones made him look Asian.

"What's the baby's name?" I asked slowly in English.

"Melvin," the woman replied.

The Ozarks have long served as a kind of sanctuary, whether an enforced one, as in the case of the Cherokees, or a voluntary one. For old-time outlaws such as Jesse James, and for latter-day criminals such as John Dillinger, the maze of hills and hollows in the Ozarks made effective hideouts. To 19th-century German immigrants, the Ozarks offered a frontier refuge from the problems of the Old World. The region still contains numerous distinctive German communities—testaments to the dream of opportunity in a new land.

In the 1970s, exiles from cities often took refuge in the Ozarks. Lured by relatively inexpensive acreage and simple living conditions, young city dwellers, many of them burned out by urban demands, removed themselves to the hills. Their plan was to set up communes and homesteads and live off the land. Usually, the back-to-the-landers came and went. The reality of extracting a living from a stubborn land undid them. Yet in most counties a few stayed.

I found some survivors in the backwoods community of Little Mulberry, in the Boston Mountains of Arkansas. I met Steve Driver, a potter from Detroit, and his wife, Louise, a weaver from Charleston, South Carolina. Farther up the dirt road live Doug and Cathy Strubel and their two teenage daughters. The Strubels arrived from Chicago in 1970 to establish a commune, one that broke up after three years. At the end of the valley is the woodworking shop of three Mexican-Americans from Houston—Manuel and David Ynosencio and Daniel

Torres—who migrated to the Ozarks because of its hardwood forests.

Most of these so-called "in-migrants" must scramble for a living. Yet many have now built homes and are raising children, and apparently they plan to stay. "The local people were instrumental in keeping us here," said Doug Strubel, a soft-spoken former computer whiz who now helps build houses. "They lent us money, provided contacts, taught us woodlore." When their commune broke up, the Strubels decided to stay because of what they viewed as Ozark values. "There's respect for individuals, respect for manual labor," Doug said. "The people don't present an image. They are what they seem to be."

Native Ozarkers helped the Drivers build their house, even though the locals were skeptical about an architectural style that incorporated asymmetrical rooflines, stained-glass windows, and a cathedral ceiling. What the in-migrants offer in return, Steve Driver says, is fresh blood. "These were derelict farms before we came," Steve said. "I think the locals were just glad to have people come back."

Under the influence of the newcomers, Little Mulberry has become a tighter community. People now come together more often, for pie suppers, barn raisings, and Fourth of July softball games. The Mexican-Americans have instituted a tamale party, usually held after the first snow. The in-migrants realize that they will always be considered outsiders. But what they have also come to learn is that Ozarkers' traditional wariness of strangers can give way to an even more fundamental trait: Ozarkers look after their neighbors.

From the valley of Little Mulberry Creek, a steep, rutted road leads up what is known locally as Gregory Mountain. Near the top lives Bill Gregory, a hog farmer. From his perch on the mountain, Bill, a gentle, heavyset man in his 60s, has watched through the years as people have come and gone. Never has it made him restless.

Bill Gregory is an Ozark native son, living on the same plot of land where he was born. He is content with his lot of raising hogs, hunting coons, and preaching at church on Sunday.

He is not without Ozark pride either. He took me in his truck to the very top of the mountain to show off something that he considers special—an Ozark field without rocks. The golden grass bent down before the truck as we drove without a bounce across the mountaintop pasture. "You can't find a rock to kill a snake with," Bill said proudly.

From his miracle of a field, we looked far into the distance at hills and valleys that rolled on and on as if nothing else existed. "I've been offered $1,500 an acre for my place," said Bill, as if to himself.

I didn't have to ask the inevitable question. "I wouldn't be any good at leaving," Bill continued, laughing softly as if incredulous at the possibility of not living on an Ozark mountain. "I wouldn't know how to act if I got anywhere else."

"If you ain't at home here, it's your fault," says Gordon Peacock, center, strumming his guitar at a music party near Ocie, Missouri. In the rural Ozarks, such parties bring families and friends together for music, food, and dancing.

PAGES 168-169: Set in an emerald Arkansas valley, the Boxley Baptist Church and Walnut Grove School manifest Ozark values little touched by time.

Mountain, Mesa,
The Four Corners

By H. Robert Morrison

Photographs by Paul Chesley

Towering higher than a 15-story building, majestic Double Arch dwarfs a visitor to the Windows section of Arches National Park north of Moab, Utah. Created when surrounding rock eroded away, such marvels in stone exemplify the many scenic wonders of the Four Corners area, the heart of the Southwest's vast, mountain-ringed Colorado Plateau.

Desert, and Canyon

As the car stalled I glanced down, hundreds of feet down the near-vertical slope high in Colorado's San Juan Mountains. I turned the key in the ignition. The starter ground, but the engine made no response. Looking back to the nearest switchback, I thought to myself, "I sure hope I don't have to back down that trail!"

This September morning I had planned to take a four-wheel-drive vehicle up narrow, winding jeep tracks from Ouray, Colorado, across 13,114-foot-high Imogene Pass, and then into the town of Telluride. I was at the beginning of a six-week exploration of the Four Corners area, the region named for the point where the boundaries of Arizona, Colorado, New Mexico, and Utah meet—the only place in the United States where four state lines converge.

During my travels in the Four Corners area I would see fresh snowfalls on mountain ghost towns and desert mesas. I would meet Indian traders and descendants of Mormon pioneers, silver miners and Native American artists. I would learn of the area's problems: Haze from Four Corners power plants hangs in the desert air; unemployment and alcoholism plague Indian reservations; mining for coal and other minerals raises land-use questions for which no easy answers exist. But mostly I would discover the incomparable beauty that makes the Four Corners area so unforgettable.

On this day I had left Ouray early in the morning and was soon bouncing along the rugged jeep trail. Although I had maps that purported to show the route over Imogene Pass, I had become confused at a fork in the trail I couldn't find on any map. Before long I found myself above the tree line, heading up a steep fall of football-size rocks. I stopped and shifted down to low gear and crawled upward. The roadway—such as it was—allowed perhaps a foot of clearance on either side of the vehicle; above were snow-dusted peaks, and below, sheer drop-offs to a mountain valley.

I saw a large rock and slowly turned to the left. Just a few inches more and I would go over the edge. Erring on the side of caution, I tried to steer too close to the rock. The right front wheel caught it, struggled to climb, and the engine stalled. I turned the key; nothing. Thinking perhaps that the engine was flooded, I waited several minutes and tried again. Still no luck. Then from above I heard the sound of a car. Creeping toward me was a light blue jeep. It halted a few feet away, and a tall bearded man got out and walked over.

"Having a bit of trouble?" he inquired mildly. I nodded.

"Sometimes they develop a vapor lock at these elevations," Raymond Williams said. "Just wait a few minutes and try again."

I did, but nothing worked. I decided to back slowly down to the nearest switchback, where I might be able to turn around, and where there was enough room to let the jeep pass. I shifted into neutral and eased off the brake. As the vehicle rapidly picked up speed, the rocky roadway threatened to wrestle the wheel away from me. I had gone only about a dozen feet before fear forced me to stop.

"Pretty scary," Raymond remarked calmly as I got out. He then offered to hook a line from the winch on the front of his jeep to my vehicle so he could provide braking power—and confidence.

"Whatever you do, don't go over the edge," Raymond said. "You're heavier than I am, and you'll pull me over along with you."

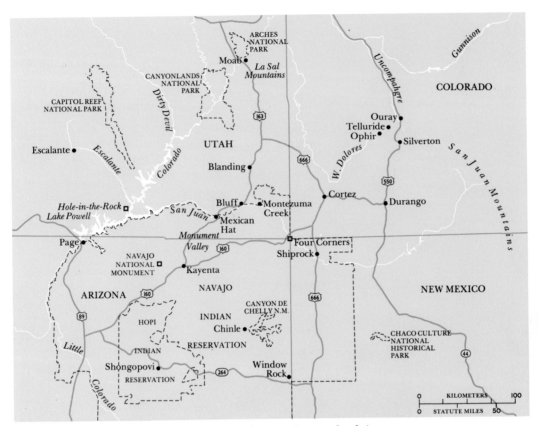

Only spot in the U. S. where four states meet, the Four Corners lends its name to a region of snow-clad peaks and haunting desert canyons. Here prehistoric cliff dwellings yield clues to the distant past; abandoned mining towns whisper of boom times in the 19th century; and Native Americans seek to preserve their heritage.

Although it seemed to take hours, I finally managed to back the quarter mile down the rough roadway. When at last I reached the switchback, my arms were sore from wrestling with the steering wheel, and my right leg ached from riding the brake. But the relief that flooded through me overwhelmed my discomfort.

I never did drive across Imogene Pass. As I headed back down the mountain, I met a man on a trail bike who told me he had ridden near the pass that morning and had been stopped by several feet of snow.

Rugged in their beauty, the San Juan Mountains bear scars of industry. They are sprinkled with mines—many of them now abandoned—and crisscrossed by jeep trails. But for this reason they are accessible to people who don't—or can't—hike or ride horses. I began my explorations of the San Juans in Ouray. Tucked into a valley, the village snuggles against cliffsides that plunge to the streets. A glance upward reveals peaks laced with waterfalls, clad in snow—scenery ever changing in sunlight and cloud, from morning to sunset.

The story of the mountains around Ouray—indeed of all the San Juans—began about 35 million years ago, when volcanic eruptions poured some 8,000 cubic miles of lava over the region. Minerals collected in fissures. During the Ice Age, *(Continued on page 179)* 173

Rumpled bulk of the San Juan Mountains hems in Telluride, Colorado. Built in the 19th-century mining era, Telluride lies at the end of the road: The single highway leading here stops at the town's outskirts. South of Telluride, rocky Palmyra Peak (right) overlooks an autumn-tinged valley.

FOLLOWING PAGES: Aglow in September sunlight, quaking aspens touch Wilson Mesa with gold as an early snowstorm boils across the distant rampart of the San Juans. In the foreground, sheep graze on the Schmidt Ranch northwest of Ophir, Colorado.

glaciers scoured out valleys and carved peaks. Following the retreat of the ice sheets, landslides exposed mineral ores—gold, silver, copper, lead, zinc. Although tapped for little more than a century, the San Juans have produced minerals worth a billion dollars at today's prices, and untold riches remain.

Just north of Ouray, I visited the Bachelor-Syracuse mine, inside Gold Hill. Although not currently in production, the mine remains

Engine 473 of the Durango & Silverton Narrow Gauge Railroad chuffs through deep snow on its daily run through the San Juans. Above, engineer Richard Connor confers with conductor R. E. Phippen. The Durango & Silverton dates to the late 1800s, when trains provided the chief link between isolated towns.

open to visitors. Astride a padded wooden beam secured to a mine car, I trailed a tiny electric engine more than three thousand feet into the mountain—and a thousand feet below the surface. Along the route my miner-guide, Tom Hash, pointed out the vein of silver ore that three bachelors had discovered in 1884—a dull gray streak about a foot wide in the ceiling of the tunnel.

"There are more than a hundred tons of high-grade ore up there," Tom said, pointing toward the ceiling, where sturdy wooden chutes held chunks of the silver-bearing rock. "However, it would cost more to ship and refine the ore than the silver is worth. We're waiting until the price of silver goes up to reopen the mine."

Like Ouray, Telluride began as a support town for the mines. In 1961, Telluride was designated a National Historic Landmark. As I walked along Main Street, it was easy for me to imagine being here in the 1880s, when the mines depended on the town for mail, supplies, and entertainment. The Sheridan Hotel has been partially restored to the grandeur it knew at the turn of the century. Not far away is a small white building that once was a bank. There a gentleman made a withdrawal without benefit of deposit—Butch Cassidy's first bank robbery.

At the edge of town runs the San Miguel River, fed by waterfalls cascading down the head of the valley. I drove one day to one of these, 365-foot-high Bridal Veil Falls. At its lip, a building juts cantilevered over the cliff. Its two-story octagonal wooden tower gives the crumbling structure the air of a castle. In reality, it is the remains of a generating station, one built in 1904 to supply alternating current electricity to the gold and silver mines. Commercial use of alternating current was pioneered here in this mountainous region of Colorado. Hydroelectricity lit the town of Telluride as early as 1891 and reduced costs in the nearby mines by more than half.

From Telluride I returned to Ouray so I could drive the scenic Million Dollar Highway toward Silverton. The original section of the highway was built in 1883 as a toll road. Today the Million Dollar Highway consists, for the most part, of two paved lanes, but the trip over it remains exciting. Few guardrails stand between the narrow shoulder and cliffs that may drop hundreds of feet. As I approached 11,075-foot Red Mountain Pass from Ouray, I saw immediately that the three peaks of Red Mountain are aptly named. A sprinkling of snow lay melting on them, and their iron oxide surfaces glowed like red enamel.

Beyond Silverton I drove through Durango and Cortez, in the southwestern corner of Colorado. Across the New Mexico border, I headed south toward the soaring stone formation of Ship Rock. Like a ghost clipper riding waves of stone, Ship Rock drew me toward the town that bears its name. I had left the mountains and entered the high mesa country, prehistoric home of the Anasazi cliff dwellers, ancestors of today's Pueblo Indians. Reservations of the Utes, Apaches, Navajos, Hopis, and other Native Americans now occupy much of this part of the Four Corners area.

In the Navajo trading town of Shiprock I met Eugene B. Joe, an artist who signs his work with his Navajo name, Baatsoslanii. Eugene paints subjects that incorporate themes from his own culture with those from earlier ones such as the Anasazi. He works in a medium he learned from his father. Eugene Joe is a sand artist.

Scholars believe the Navajos may have learned sand painting from other Indians during the 17th century. Whatever the source, the art today has evolved into a complex, integral part of many Navajo religious ceremonies. With a renewed interest in traditional art, modern Navajo artists sought ways to preserve their designs. In the late 1940s they began using glue to fix the sand to a wooden background.

A handsome man with a quick smile and shining black hair falling below his shoulders, Eugene invited me into his studio to show me how he paints with sand. "It begins with finding the various colors of rock," he said. "We gather chunks and bring them home to dry thoroughly— you can't tell a rock's true color until it's really dry. Then we break them up with a hammer. We used to grind them with a mortar and pestle. Now we use an old coffee grinder. Finally, we sift the sand; if it's too powdery or too coarse we can't use it."

He picked up a painting. Partially completed shapes adhered to a base of particle board that had been coated with a film of glue, dusted with beige sand, and left to dry. Eugene swirled a fine brush in a jar of water, shook off the excess, and dipped its tip into a container of glue—white household glue, he told me, diluted with a little water and with a secret ingredient or two added.

Bending over his work, he added a row of fine dots along the edge of a butterfly's wing; each dot was hardly bigger than a period in this book. Holding a pinch of turquoise-colored sand between thumb and forefinger, he expertly dusted a fine line along the dots of glue.

"I have to wait for the glue to set before shaking off the excess sand and going on to another color or another part of the painting," he said. "That's one reason it may take several weeks to complete even a small painting. But it also gives you time to think while you're working.

"When I was a small boy, my grandfather told me, 'Do not run with the times. Walk with the sun.' I didn't understand what he meant at the time. Now I do. That's my philosophy of life now."

Even more than for their sand paintings, the Navajos are known for their handcrafted silver necklaces, belts, bracelets, and other jewelry, much of which incorporates large pieces of turquoise. Silversmith Joe Kieyoomia agreed to show me his craft. When I arrived at his home about a mile from the Little Water Trading Post south of Shiprock, Joe had set up his workbench in his tidy living room. As I watched, he laid a sheet of silver on his anvil, carefully positioned a stamp on the sheet, then gave it a mighty whack with a hammer. Lifting the stamp, he

Revered by Indians and a landmark for pioneers, craggy Ship Rock looms above the desert floor at the end of a razor-backed ridge. The 1,800-foot-high formation rises in northwestern New Mexico, on the Navajo Indian Reservation.

showed me the starburst design imprinted in the silver. "I made all my stamps myself," he said. "This one came from a piece of steel I picked up at a garage while I was waiting for my pickup to be fixed. I noticed it lying half-buried in the ground outside and thought it might work into a tool. The garage owner gave it to me; I took it home, filed the design into it, and I've used it ever since."

With the design stamped into the silver, *(Continued on page 188)*

Steady hands of Navajo artist Eugene B. Joe and his aunt Lillie Joe Hatathley create art from sand near the town of Shiprock, New Mexico. They work inside a hogan—a traditional one-room circular dwelling made of logs and adobe. Eugene's father, James, once a practicing medicine man, watches the symbol of renewal at right take shape. Such paintings figure in many Navajo ceremonies. Opposite, Lillie Joe Hatathley stands framed by the doorway of the hogan.

182

183

Vaulted alcove of sandstone encloses Betatakin—Navajo for "Ledge House"—at Navajo National Monument west of Kayenta, Arizona (right). This 135-room complex, built and abandoned between A.D. 1250 and 1300, housed Anasazi, "the ancient ones," ancestors of today's Pueblo Indians. The structures below may have served as storehouses for food raised by the inhabitants of Betatakin.

Hopi artists look to their heritage for inspiration: Neil David, Sr., (left) holds the partially carved figure of a Kwahu, or eagle, Kachina, a supernatural being in traditional Hopi belief. Below, Michael Kabotie's studio reflects his varied talents—among them painting and fashioning silver and gold jewelry. Two of his works in progress (bottom) rest on the plan for a figure he adapted from early Hopi murals.

Joe scribed a circle around it and then cut it out with a jeweler's saw. Filing the edge smooth, he placed the circle of silver, about the size of a quarter, over a depression in a block of steel, positioned another tool on it, and struck the tool several times. Lifting up the silver, now somewhat cone-shaped, Joe explained that he would make another piece like it and solder the edges of the two together. Holes drilled into the silver would complete his work on a single bead for a necklace, which might have 50 or more beads and sell for more than $500.

Leaving Shiprock, I headed to the southeast, toward Chaco Canyon. A sign where a dirt road met the highway warned against taking heavy trailers to Chaco Culture National Historical Park or attempting the drive during rainy weather. I reached Chaco Canyon some 30 dusty, bouncing miles later and pitched my tent in the campground.

The next day I explored the Anasazi ruins of Chaco Canyon, great stone apartment complexes of which the best-known is Pueblo Bonito, whose development can be traced from about A.D. 1030 to 1079. At its zenith, Pueblo Bonito stood five stories high, housed an estimated one thousand people, and contained perhaps 650 rooms. Of these, at least 37 were kivas, sunken circular chambers like those still used by the Hopis and other pueblo dwellers of the Southwest.

Across the canyon from Pueblo Bonito lies Casa Rinconada, site of the largest kiva found in Chaco Canyon. There I made my way down a narrow stone staircase—once a covered, cramped passageway—and emerged into the great chamber whose floor measures 63½ feet in diameter. I was intrigued to learn that on the summer solstice the rising sun shines through a window and precisely illuminates one of the 28 evenly spaced niches in the kiva wall. Was this astronomical alignment deliberate? Some investigators believe so, although the remains of walls outside the kiva window indicate that a structure might have stood there which could have blocked the sunlight—unless that room, too, had a properly aligned window. We may never know for sure.

I saw additional ruins at Canyon de Chelly—pronounced "da-shay"—National Monument, just outside Chinle, Arizona. With a Navajo guide, I drove into the canyon, where sandstone walls, like tapestries with dark streaks, rise in places a thousand feet above the ruins of Anasazi cliff dwellings. On the floor of the canyon lie Navajo farms and ranches, continuing a span of human occupancy here that reaches back some 20 centuries.

The sandy beds of the streams running through the canyon serve as treacherous roadways. Where the sand is dry and loose a car can almost instantly lose traction and become mired down to the axles. Wet surfaces conceal pools of quicksand; a park ranger told me that dozens of cars and trucks had sunk without a trace into these streambeds.

Impressive as the cliff dwellings and the towering canyon walls were, what most interested me were the pictographs my guide pointed out. Some were prehistoric, some done by the Navajos. At Standing Cow Ruin, a particularly striking panel depicts a Spanish cavalry unit accompanied by a priest in vestments clearly distinguished by a cross.

Swirl of sandstone records the might of rushing water: Centuries of flash floods carved this narrow canyon on the Navajo Reservation east of Page, Arizona.

On the Hopi Reservation, an enclave entirely surrounded by the larger Navajo Reservation, I was happy to see my friend Michael Kabotie, near the village of Shongopovi. I had met Michael, a well-known artist and poet, on a previous visit here. Like Eugene Joe, Michael seeks to reinterpret his ancestral heritage by using traditional motifs in his own way. I was especially taken with a serigraph—a silk screen print—Michael had done as a self-portrait. In it, his features blend and merge with the stonework of an Anasazi wall.

Explained Michael, "I was trying to express the closeness I feel to the heritage handed down to me from countless past generations."

In a land of towering buttes and sweeping desert vistas such as those at Canyon de Chelly, Monument Valley still stands out. This 29,816-acre tract straddling the Arizona-Utah border was set aside in 1958 by the Navajo Tribal Council. Today it is administered and protected by the Recreational Resources Department of the Navajo Nation. Here bizarre shapings of weathered rock and earth immediately aroused my curiosity. How could a land ever come to look like this?

Geologists believe this section of the Four Corners area once consisted of sand washed down from the early Rocky Mountains some 200 million years ago. The pressures of later deposits cemented the individual sand grains together to form rock. A gradual uplift of the land, caused by pressure from within the earth, split and cracked the surface. Some of the rock layers, especially those near the edges of uplifted areas, were sharply tilted. Flash floods, frost, and rainstorms widened and deepened valleys and streambeds into canyons; where caps of harder rock protected softer layers below, pillars and buttes remained towering above the valley floor.

A graded dirt road leads to the floor of Monument Valley. Some of the red sandstone formations are named for shapes they resemble: the two Mittens; an astonishingly realistic Elephant Butte. There's also a John Ford's Point, named for the director of *Stagecoach*, the first of many Hollywood movies filmed in Monument Valley.

I left the Navajo Reservation at the settlement of Mexican Hat, Utah, where a bridge spans the San Juan River. Just a few miles away is the village of Bluff, whose story began in the 1870s. At that time, Mormon leaders in Salt Lake City had become concerned about the safety of settlements in southern Utah territory because of an increase in Indian raids and white outlawry there. The leaders sent out a call for pioneers. Their object was to establish a mission on the San Juan River, which they hoped would foster friendly relations with the Indians and help bring law and order to the region.

"Yes, my father was one of the pioneers of the San Juan Mission, as Bluff was called at first." Lynn Lyman spoke as I sat with him and his wife, Hazel, in their living room in Blanding, not far from Bluff. A tall man in his 70s, Lynn has broad shoulders and powerful hands that testify to a lifetime of hard work.

"At the time, nobody knew much of anything about this area," he continued. "The earliest European explorers, the Escalante expedition of 1776, avoided the rough, canyon-slashed desert badlands, and later adventurers mostly followed in their footsteps."

Even a Mormon scouting party that decided on a site for the new mission got there by swinging south through Hopi villages rather than attempting to cross the rugged terrain that lay between existing settlements and the San Juan River. The scouts then returned via the northern Escalante route. The site they chose for the mission was near present-day Montezuma Creek 22 miles east of Bluff.

By October of 1879 the Mormon settlers were ready to leave their assembly point, the frontier village of Escalante, about 125 miles to the west. The line of Mormon wagons—83 in all—stretched for more than two miles, followed by a huge train of livestock. Some 250 men, women, and children began the trip. The scouts' report of the difficulties they encountered prompted the expedition leaders to reject both the southern route through Hopi lands and the northern route along the Escalante Trail. Winter was approaching, and the leaders hoped to reach the San Juan before the worst weather set in. Therefore, they decided to strike eastward and find their own shortcut.

"That was probably the worst decision they could have made," Lynn reflected. Ahead of them lay some of the most difficult and demanding terrain in North America. The first major obstacle for the expedition was the canyon of the Colorado River. Scouts found a narrow notch in the west wall of the canyon a thousand feet above the water. Dubbed "Hole-in-the-Rock," this spot gave its name to the expedition and to the trail. For weeks the men labored to make a wagon road down to the river. At one point they drilled holes in the rock face, wedged oak posts into the holes, and laid a roadway of brush, earth, and rocks across the posts. While they worked, another crew across the Colorado blasted and dug another roadway up the 250-foot-high sheer cliffs east of the river.

By the end of January the company had crossed the Colorado. Wagons were ferried; livestock swam. The Hole-in-the-Rock expedition overcame obstacle after obstacle as the weeks dragged on into bitter winter. The myth of the "shortcut" was gradually forgotten; no choice remained but to press on. By late March the exhausted men, women, children, and animals encountered the last great barrier between them and their destination: Comb Ridge, a wall of sandstone a thousand feet high running 30 miles north from the San Juan River. With no way around it, the Mormons built a road up the Comb at a spot they christened San Juan Hill.

*L*ynn and Hazel Lyman drove me in their jeep to San Juan Hill. We paused at its base. Lynn pointed out traces of the roadway remaining, and we started following it. About two-thirds of the way up, the jeep could go no farther. Lynn and I continued to the top on foot, walking over wheel tracks chipped into the rock to help keep the wagons upright. Here and there, jumbled rocks still show where the Mormons had built up the roadbed.

In his journal, Lynn's uncle noted of San Juan Hill, ". . . we have to do some work to get up over the bench." That was understatement; it took seven teams to pull one wagon up that hill. Another man recalled, ". . . the worst stretches could easily be identified by the dried blood and matted hair from the forelegs of the struggling teams."

By early April of 1880, most of the wagons had reached the bottomlands of the San Juan. Montezuma Creek, their original goal, lay less than 25 miles away by easy dirt trail. To the exhausted pioneers, it was too far. "I was so tired and sore," one woman recalled, "that I had no desire to be any place except where I was." And there they founded the San Juan Mission, today the town of Bluff. Miraculously, not a single life was lost, and every wagon reached the mission.

Marveling at the saga of the Mormon trek, I continued to explore Utah's rugged canyon country. At Capitol Reef National Park, I drove toward seldom-visited Cathedral Valley. As I stood at an overlook, park ranger Andy Ferguson drove up. He introduced himself, and we chatted for a few minutes. "Don't miss Glass Mountain," Andy told me. "It's well signposted; you can't miss it."

Andy's prediction held true. In Cathedral Valley, not far from the stone pinnacles of the Temple of the Sun, I easily found Glass Mountain. Its dome of crystalline gypsum, glittering under a film of red dust, rose abruptly from the valley floor. The term "mountain" is something of an exaggeration—it's only about 15 feet high. But the formation is surprising in its clarity. I picked up an eighth-inch-thick chip weathered from the dome and held it against a newspaper. I could easily read the print through it.

To the east, Canyonlands National Park cuts a maze of channels through the Colorado Plateau. Much of the park is virtually inaccessible except by helicopter. In the relatively developed areas most roads remain unpaved. Four-wheel-drive trails lead to a small number of observation points. Even for someone on foot, sheer canyon walls and drop-offs present a difficulty; a backpacker would have to carry a prohibitively heavy load of water to hike for any length of time.

"You can stand within 500 feet of water and die of thirst there," goes a saying, "because the water's straight down a canyon wall."

Driving an automobile here requires careful planning. Island in the Sky, in the northern section of Canyonlands, lies miles from the nearest supply of gasoline, in Moab. Driving from Moab to this section and back is more than a hundred-mile trip.

I checked my fuel gauge as I left Moab before sunrise one morning. Orion and the Pleiades faded as the cloud-streaked sky brightened from black to navy blue. I parked in a turnoff at The Neck, a narrow strip of mesa once fenced across by cowboys to keep in their herds.

In the distance to the southeast, a pink glow gradually enveloped the snowy peaks of the La Sal Mountains. Below the mesa where I stood, canyon-cut mazes grew more distinct as the sky lightened through shades of rose to blue. Far below me a red-tailed hawk soared on the morning breezes. The Colorado River rolled onward, still in shadow. In the layered canyon walls time itself seemed visible.

I was at the end of my stay in the Four Corners area, yet I knew I had hardly begun to experience its manifold wonders. That could take a lifetime and more, for here in this colossal landscape of mountain, mesa, desert, and canyon, the only things to rival the marvels of today are those awaiting discovery tomorrow.

Stylized mountain sheep lifts its head on a rock wall near the San Juan River west of Bluff, Utah. Carved by Anasazi, the figure may represent a prayer for an increase of game or memorialize a successful hunt.

Twisting through a tortured landscape, the Dirty Devil River snakes toward Lake Powell in southeastern Utah. On the horizon, snowy peaks of the Henry Mountains punctuate the sere red hues of surrounding mesas and buttes.

FOLLOWING PAGES: Sunrise rekindles a scene 25 million years in the making—the majestic pinnacles of Monument Valley. Straddling the Arizona-Utah border on the northern edge of the Navajo Reservation, Monument Valley captures the essence of America's hidden corners. In its recesses the winds still sing an ageless song of nature and of freedom.

Notes on Contributors

LESLIE ALLEN was born in Washington, D. C., and grew up in Europe, Asia, and South America. A member of the Special Publications staff since 1978, she wrote a chapter on Tierra del Fuego in *Secret Corners of the World* and a chapter on maritime preservation in *Preserving America's Past*.

NATHAN BENN has been a contract photographer for NATIONAL GEOGRAPHIC since 1972, working on subjects as diverse as medicinal plants in Asia and Africa and ethnic minorities in the United States. He was a contributor to the Special Publications *Nature's Healing Arts* and *Isles of the Caribbean*.

Free lance MATT BRADLEY, a resident of Little Rock, Arkansas, discovered photography as a U. S. Air Force pilot. His assignments for the Society have included the March 1977 magazine article on the Buffalo National River and a chapter for the Special Publication *America's Wild and Scenic Rivers*.

JIM BRANDENBURG became a contract photographer for NATIONAL GEOGRAPHIC in 1978. His most recent assignments include work in China, the Soviet Union, and South Africa. Jim was voted the National Press Photographers Association Magazine Photographer of the Year in 1980 and in 1982.

Free-lance photographer PAUL CHESLEY contributes regularly to NATIONAL GEOGRAPHIC and has photographed Death Valley, the Sawtooth Range, and the Continental Divide for Special Publications. Paul, who lives in Aspen, Colorado, covered the natural splendors of Europe for *Nature's World of Wonders*.

A resident of Louisville, Kentucky, free-lance photographer DAN DRY was named the National Press Photographers Association Newspaper Photographer of the Year in 1981. His work has appeared in a number of books and national magazines, including *Time* and *Newsweek*.

LOWELL GEORGIA spent two years as a picture editor for the Society and has worked as a free-lance photographer for the magazine and Special Publications for more than a decade. A resident of Arvada, Colorado, he photographed the Special Publication *Into the Wilderness* and contributed to *Trails West*.

On assignment for Special Publications, free-lance photographer ANNIE GRIFFITHS has covered the north woods of Minnesota for *Exploring America's Backcountry*, the Colorado Rockies for *America's Magnificent Mountains*, and rural preservation for *Preserving America's Past*. She lives in Minneapolis.

Before coming to the Society in 1958, MARY ANN HARRELL earned a B.A. in English at Wellesley College and an M.A. at the University of North Carolina. Assignments for Special Publications have taken her to East Africa, Australia, the Caribbean, and South Pacific islands.

CHRISTINE ECKSTROM LEE joined the Society in 1974. She has written chapters in *Mysteries of the Ancient World*, *Exploring America's Backcountry*, *Isles of the Caribbean*, and *Peoples and Places of the Past*. The coauthor of *America's Atlantic Isles*, she will contribute to the upcoming *Exploring America's Valleys*.

H. ROBERT MORRISON, a graduate of Howard University, joined the Society in 1964. As a member of the Special Publications staff he has contributed to a number of book projects, including *Mysteries of the Ancient World* and *The Ocean Realm*. He was the coauthor of *America's Atlantic Isles*.

A native of Champaign, Illinois, THOMAS O'NEILL joined the National Geographic Society staff in 1976. He has written about the canyons of the Southwest, the Florida Everglades, and the Canadian wilderness for Special Publications. He was the author of *Back Roads America: A Portfolio of Her People*.

With an archaeology background, staff writer GENE S. STUART coauthored the Special Publications *Discovering Man's Past in the Americas* and *The Mysterious Maya*. She wrote *The Mighty Aztecs*, contributed to *Mysteries of the Ancient World* and *Preserving America's Past*, and has written several children's books.

SUZANNE VENINO grew up in New Jersey and later moved to Washington, D. C., where she graduated from George Washington University. On Special Publications' staff since 1977, she has written a number of children's books and will contribute to the forthcoming *Exploring America's Scenic Highways*.

ANNIE GRIFFITHS

Whimsical sign in northern Nevada's Great Basin country proclaims the spirit of those who live in places off the beaten path.

HARDCOVER STAMP: Pasqueflowers bloom on the northern prairie.

DRAWING BY JODY BOLT, FROM A PHOTOGRAPH BY JIM BRANDENBURG.

Acknowledgments

The Special Publications Division is grateful to the individuals, groups, and organizations named and quoted in the text and to those cited here for their generous assistance during the preparation of this book: Andy Anderson, Donald R. Baugh, Phil Bjork, Eirik A. T. Blom, Bridgett Boulton, Ray Brassieur, Earline Broussard, Sandra Buchman, Robert H. Burgess, Douglas Childs, Buddy M. Corbett, Jay Custer, Amy J. Dansie, Robert G. Elston, Ralph E. Eshelman, James Eskridge, Mac Frimodig, Russel L. Gerlach, Jon L. Gibson, Robert Gramling, Steven M. Greenhut, Norman Harrington, Tom Hooper, Donald B. Hurlbut, William Jabine II, Paula Johnson, Edward Joubert, Robert Le Blanc, Betty Lombardi, James P. Ludwig, Richard E. McCamant, John David McFarland, William K. McNeil, Bob Macomber, Murray T. Mahan, D. L. Menard, Mike Mills, Ann Moore, Allen Newberry, Charles Oscar Noble, Milton Rafferty, Revon Reed, Chandler S. Robbins, Robin D. Shaddox, Robert Skuggen, Kenneth L. Smith, Dennis Sotola, Sharon Edaburn Taylor, John O. Thomas, Gary Tucker, Donald R. Tuohy, Calvin Turnbow, Jerry D. Vineyard, Scott Wassamund, John E. Wylie.

Index

Boldface indicates illustrations
Italic refers to picture captions

Aaron, Order of: Utah 22, **22-23**
Acadians *123*, 125 *see also* Cajuns
Alligators 133, 135, 137
Alta Toquima, Nev. 11, **12**, 18
Amargosa Opera House, Death Valley Junction, Calif. 28, **29**
Anasazi Indians: art 180, 188, **191**; ruins *173*, 180, **184, 185**, 188
Arches National Park, Utah **170-171**
Arizona: canyons 188, **188**; national monuments **184, 185**, 188; rock formations 188, 189, **194-195**
Arkansas Ozarks **1**, **144-145**, 146, 147, *147*, **154**, 155, **155**, 156, **158-163**, 165, 166, **168-169**
Atchafalaya Basin, La. 124

Badgers **81**, 85
Badlands: buttes 64, **90-91**; map **65**; name origin 64; natural history 64, *65*, *66*, 70, 79; rock formations 64, **66-67**, 79, **82-83**, 85, **90-91**
Badlands National Park, S. Dak. **82-83**, 85, 86
Bartelli, Ingrid Mattson and Leonard 99, 104
Bay Mills Chippewa Reservation, Mich.: powwow 105, **108**, 111
Bears 78, *96*, 98, 112
Beaver Creek, Mo. 157, 164
Becket, Marta 28, **28**, **29**
Belvedere (mansion), Pass Christian, Miss. **135**
Betatakin (ruins), Ariz. **184, 185**
Birches, white 94, **100**
Birds 26, 54, 78, **80-81**, **84**, 85, 98, 112, 113, 124-126, 191; water birds *74*, **75**, **77-79**, 118, 124, 137, **140-141**, waterfowl 48, *50*, **50**, 53, 54, *72*, 125, *133*
Bison 65, 85-86, **90-91**
Bittern, American **79**
Black Hills, S. Dak.-Wyo. *65*, 79
Blackwater National Wildlife Refuge, Md. **50**, 53-54
Bluff, Utah: history 189-191
Boats **34-35**, 36, *37*, 43, **46**, 58, 87, **114-115**, 137; canoes 95, 98, **162-163**, 164, pirogue **128**; handcrafted 55, 125, **128-129**; mail carriers 42, 134-136, **136**; skipjacks **44-45**, 54-55; *see also* Ferries; Shipwrecks
Bodie State Historic Park, Calif. **30-33**
Boston Mountains, Ark.: community 165-166; forest *159*
Boudreaux, Eddie 125, **129**
Boxley Baptist Church, Ark. **168**
Bridal Veil Falls, Colo. **7**, 180
Brimley, Mich.: centennial 105, **109**
Buffalo River, Ark. **162-163**

Cajuns **125**, **128**, **129**; fishing 124-125, **128-129**, 133, 136; healers 126, 133;

history *123*, 125; hunting 124-125, 133, *133*; marriage practices **127**; musicians **130-131**, *131*, 133
California: ghost towns **30-33**, renewal 28, *28*; gold discovery 20, *31*
Camping 11, 18, 124-125, **162-163**
Canyon de Chelly National Monument, Ariz. 188, 189
Canyonlands National Park, Utah 191
Capitol Reef National Park, Utah 191
Captiva Island, Fla. 136-137
Casa Rinconada (kiva), N. Mex. 188
Cathedral Gorge State Park, Nev. **24**
Cattle ranches *20*, 27, 64, 65, 71, 79, 86-87, *86*, 124
Cayler Prairie, Iowa 88
Chaco Canyon, N. Mex. 188
Chaco Culture National Historical Park, N. Mex. 188
Cherokee Indians **157**, 164-165
Chesapeake Bay, and region: agriculture 36, *37*, 49, 55; birds 48, *50*, **50**, 53-54; bridge 36; churches 42-43, **43**, 59, 55, 59; crafts 48, 55, 59; dimensions 36, *37*; environmental problems 36, 48-49, 54; history 36, 37, 42, 49; hunting 36, 48, **50-51**, **52**, **53**, 54, 58; map **37**; natural history 36, eroded islands 49; tributaries 36, *47*; watermen **34-35**, 36, *39*, **40**, 42, 43, **44-46**, 48, 49, 54, 55, 58, 59; western shore 36, **46-47**; *see also* Eastern Shore; Smith Island; Tangier Island
Chestertown, Md.: fox hunting **52, 53**
Chippewa Indians 94-95; powwow 105, **108**, 111
Churches 42-43, **43**, 59, 70, 99, **114-115**, 165, 168
Clark, Merle 70
Cliff dwellings *173*, 180, **184, 185**, 188
Coal 64; mines 70
Colorado: minerals and mining *6*, 173, *175*, 179, 180; mountains 172-173, **174-178**; national historic landmark *6*, **174-175**, 179, 180; railroad **178**, **179**; waterfalls **7**, 179-180
Colorado River, U. S. 190, 191
Copper 94, 179; mines 25, 98, 99
Cormorants 137, **140-141**
Costumes: circus 105, **109**; frontier **68-69**, **144-145**; Halloween **59**
Crab Derby, Crisfield, Md. **38-39**
Crabs and crabbing 36, *39*, **40**, 42, 48, 59, 136; soft-shell crabs **41**, 43
Crisfield, Md. **38-39**, 42, 43
Curry, Martha Drummond 58-59
Cypress trees **122-123**, 124

Dancers and dancing 64, *69*, 71, 148, 155, 165, *166*; ballet 28, **29**; Cajun *126*, **128**; powwows 64, 86, 105, *109*, 111
Dartez family 126, 133
Davis, Jefferson 134
Death Valley Junction, Calif. 28, *28*
Deer Lake, Mich. **2-3**
Dianas Punch Bowl (crater), Nev. **14-15**
Dickey, N. Dak.: centennial **68-69**

Dinosaur fossils 79
Dirty Devil River, Utah **192-193**
Dollar Bay, Mich. **110**
Double Arch, Utah **170-171**
Driver, Louise and Steve 165, 166
Drug Enforcement Administration (DEA) 156
Ducks 48, *50*, 53, 54, 125
Dufurrena family 27
Durango & Silverton Narrow Gauge Railroad, Colo. **178, 179**

Eagles, 25, 26, 54
Eastern Shore, Md.-Va. 36, 42, 49, **50-51**, 55, **56-57**, 58
"Elephant Land" (rock formations), Nev. **16-17**, 19
EskDale, Utah: religious community **22-23**
The Everglades, Fla.: wildlife 137
Ewell, Md.: Methodism 42-43, **43**
Ewen, Mich.: logging festival 105, **109**

Fayette, Mich.: historic park 99
Fern, maidenhair **159**
Ferries 111; paddle-wheel 87-88
Festivals *39*, **68-69**, 105, **108**, **109**, 126, **128**; parades **38-39**, **68**, 105, *109*
Fishing 87, 113, 124, 125, 133, 136, 164; brook trout **102-103**, 112; industry 124, **128-129** *see also* Watermen
Floden, Jennings 79
Florida: beaches 136, **138-140**; mangrove islands 137, **140-143**; panhandle **138-139**
Four Corners: agriculture 188; archaeological sites *173*, 180, **184, 185**, 188, **191**; buttes 189, **192-193**; canyons *173*, 188, **188**, 189-191, **192-193**; crafts 181, **186, 187**, 188; deserts 172, **181**, 189; forests **175-178**; history 172, *181*, 189-191; map **173**; mesas 172, **176-177**, 180, 191, **192-193**; mountains *170*, *172*-173, *173*, **174-178**, 179, 180, 191; name origin 172, *173*; national monuments **184, 185**, 188, 189; national parks **170-171**, 191; natural history *170*, *173*, 179, *188*, 189; ranches **176-177**, 188
Frémont, John C. 20

Galveston, Texas: storm (1900) 119
Geese 48, 59; Canada **50**, 53, 54, 98
General stores **1**, 26, 125-126, **151**
Ghost towns **30-33**, 104-105, 172; renewal 28, *28*
Gibbs, Robert 137
Ginseng root 156
Glass, Mike 85, 86
Glass Mountain, Utah 191
Gold 20, 118, 119, 179, *187*; mines *6*, 25, 79, 180
Grand Island, Mich. **106-107**
Great Basin: archaeological sites **8-9**, 10, 11, **12**; area 10; arts 28, **29**; desert *10*, 18, 19, *25*, 28; ghost towns **30-33**, renewal 28, *28*; history 20;

hot springs **13-15;** maps **10,** 18, 20;
mining 18, **18,** 20, 25-28, *31;*
mountains 10, *10,* 11, **12,** 19, 20, 25,
26, 28; myths 20; name origin 10,
10, 20; natural history *25;* ranches
21, 27; religious communities 20,
22, **22-23;** rock formations **16-17,**
19, **24;** valleys 10, 11, **21,** 27
Grebes *74,* **74, 75**
Gregory, Bill 166
Grimes Point Archaeological Area,
near Fallon, Nev. **8-9**
Guidry, Jeb, and family 126, 133
Guirard, Greg 124-125
Gulf Coast: agriculture 124-126, **125;**
barrier islands **116-117,** 118-119,
120, **120,** 124, 136-137; bayou *123,*
125, **128-129;** beaches **116-117, 120,**
133, **138-140;** fishing 124, 125, **128-**
129, 136; history 118, 119, *119, 123,*
135; length 118, *119;* mailman 134-
136, **136;** mangrove islands 137,
140-143; map *120,* 124, 137; parks *120,*
124, 137; ranches 119, 124;
shipwrecks 118; storms 118, 119,
124, 134-136; swamps *117,* 124,
125, 137; wildlife 124, 125, 133,
135, 137, birds 118, 124-126, *133,*
137, **140-141**

Harrington, Len **130-131,** *131,* 133
Harris, Richard 119, 124
Hatoff, Brian 11, **12, 13, 15,** 18
Hawks **80-81,** 85, 112, 191
Hebert, Maxie 125-126
Hellickson, Micki 65, 70
Henry Mountains, Utah **192-193**
Heritage Festival: Loreauville, La. **128**
Hikers and hiking 11, **12, 15, 97, 101**
Hodgson Mill, Ozark County, Mo. **149**
Holt, Bob 148, 155, 164
Homesteading *62,* 70, 104, **160-161,**
165-166; sod buildings 64, **71,** 87, 88
Hopi Indians 188, 190; artists **186,**
187, 189; reservation 180, 189
Horseback riding **53,** 65, 85-87, **116**
Hunters and hunting 36, 48, **50-51,**
52, 53, 54, 58, 78, 113, 124-125, **132,**
133, *133,* **150,** *151,* 156-157, *159,*
164, 166
Hydroelectric power 87; historic
generating station **7,** 180

Ice Age glaciers 36, *72,* 88, 104, 112,
147, 173, 179
Illinois Ozarks 146, *147*
Imogene Pass, Colo. 172-173
Indians *9,* 10, 26, 48, 70, 87, **89,** 118,
119, 124, 137, 172, *173;* art 19, 172,
180-181, **182, 183, 186, 187,** 188,
189, **191;** Old Copper Culture 98;
religion *88,* 94-95, 165, 180-181,
182, 187; Trail of Tears 165; *see also*
Cherokee; Chippewa; Osage;
Shoshone; Sioux
Iowa: prairies 64, 88
Iron 99; mines 25

J. N. "Ding" Darling Wildlife Refuge,

Sanibel Island, Fla. 137
James, Clifford 134-136, **136**
Jefferson, Mount, Nev. 11, **12**
Jewelry, Indian 181, **187,** 188
Joe, Eugene B. 180-181, **182,** 189
Johanson, Bruce 94, 105
Jubilees 136

Kabotie, Michael **187,** 189
Kansas Ozarks 146, *147*
Keweenaw Bay, Mich. **113**
Keweenaw Peninsula, Mich. 98, 99
Kieyoomia, Joe 181, 188
Kliber, Jim 95, 98

Larks, horned **84**
Lead 179; mines 25, 156
Little Carp River, Mich. **97**
Little Missouri River: badlands 64, 65,
66-67, 70
Little Mulberry, Ark. 165, 166
Log Jam-bor-ee, Ewen, Mich. 105, **109**
Lombardo, Al **18,** 25-26
Longfellow, Henry Wadsworth 94,
123, 125
Longfellow-Evangeline State
Commemorative Area, St.
Martinville, La. **122-123**
Longfellow House, near Pascagoula,
Miss. 134
Loreauville, La.: festival **128**
Louisiana: agriculture 124, 125, **125;**
Cajuns *123,* 124-126, **125, 127-131,**
133, *133;* hunting 124-125, **132,**
133; park **122-123**
Lumber industry 99, 156; logging *95,*
104, 105, 112, 113
Lyman, Hazel and Lynn 189, 190

McCann, Gordon 148, 164
Mackinac Island, Mich. 111-112, **114-**
115
McLane, Alvin **16, 17,** 18-19
Mamou, La.: marriage practices **127**
Mangrove islands 137, **140-143**
Mansions 55, **56-57,** 58, 99, 134, **135**
Maps: badlands and prairies **65;**
Chesapeake Bay, and region **37;**
Four Corners **173;** Great Basin **10,**
18, 20; Gulf Coast **118-119;** Ozarks
147; Upper Peninsula 94, **95**
Marijuana 156
Marmarth, N. Dak. 70-71
Marquette, Mich. **101,** 113
Marshall, Paul 48
Marshes 36, 37, *37,* 42, 48, 49, **50,** 53,
54, **60-61,** *117,* 125, **132,** 133, 137;
pothole marshes **72-79**
Mattson, Greg 112-113
May, Mickey 87-88
Meaux, La. 125-126
Michigan *see* Upper Peninsula
Minerals and mining: Four Corners *6,*
172, 173, *173, 175,* 179, 180; Great
Basin **18,** 20, 25-28, *31;* North
Dakota 64, 70; Ozarks 156; South
Dakota 79; Upper Peninsula *92, 95,*
98, 99, 111, 112
Miner's Castle, Pictured Rocks

National Lakeshore, Mich. **101**
Minnesota: prairies 64, *72*
Mississippi: man-made beach 133;
mansions 134, **135;** slave trade 134
Missouri Ozarks 146, *147,* 148, **149-**
153, 156, 157, 164, **167**
Missouri River: man-made lakes 87
Mobile Bay, Ala.: Eastern Shore
mailman 134-136, **136**
Monitor Valley, Nev. **13-15**
Monument Valley, Ariz.-Utah 189,
194-195
Mormons: Utah 20, *22,* 172, 189-191
Mountain View, Ark.: folk center **144-**
145; wood carvings **154, 155**
Munising, Mich.: harbor *104*
Murphy, Wadie 54, 55
Mushrooms 112; fly agaric **96**
Music and musicians 64, 71, **111,** 113;
bands **39,** 105; Cajun **130-131,** *131,*
133; children **22-23;** Indian 86, 105,
111; Ozark *144,* 147, 148, 155, 165,
167
Mystic Theater, Marmarth, N. Dak. 71

Navajo Indians 180-181, **182-183,**
188, 189; reservation 180, 189
Navajo National Monument, Ariz.
184, 185
Navarre Beach, Fla. **138-139**
Nebraska: agriculture **62-63;**
community life 87; prairies 64; sand
dunes 87
Nevada: archaeological areas **8-9,** 11,
12; hot springs **13-15;** mining **18,**
25, 26; rock formations **16-17,** 19,
24
New Mexico: rock formations 180,
181; ruins 188
Newton County, Ark. 156, *159*
North Dakota: agriculture **72-73;**
badlands 64, 65, **66-67;** coal 64, 70;
festival **68-69;** national park 65, **66-**
67, 70; oil 70; prairies 64, 70-71, **72-**
73; wildlife 86
Nousiainen, George **111,** 113

Oahe, Lake, S. Dak. 87
Ocie, Mo.: music party **167**
Oil 70; rigs 113, 119, 126
Oklahoma Ozarks 146, *147;* Indians
157, *159,* 164-165
Osage Indians *159,* 164
Ouray, Colo. *173,* 179
Outlaws 165, 179, 189
Oysters and oystering 36, *43,* **44-46,**
48, **49,** 54, 55, 59
Ozark Folk Center, Mountain View,
Ark. **144-145**
Ozark National Forest, Ark. *159*
Ozarks: agriculture *159,* **160-161,**
livestock 156, 166; boundaries 146,
147, *147;* crafts *144,* 146, **154, 155,**
165-166; exotic crops 156;
footbridge **150;** forests 147, 156,
157, **158-161,** 166; highest point
147; history 156, 157, *159,* 165;
hunting **150,** *151,* 156-157, *159,*
164, 166; isolation 147-148; map

147; mills **149**, 156; name origin
156; parks 146, **162-163**; valleys
158, 160-161, *161*, 166, **168-169;**
way of life *144*, 146-148, *151*, *153*,
155-157, *161*, 164-166

Padre Island, Texas: beaches **116-117**,
118, **120**; history 119, 124; length
119, *120*, 124; wind-surfing **121**
Padre Island National Seashore,
Texas *120*, 124
Palmyra Peak, Colo. **175**
Pasqueflowers **84, 85**
Pass Christian, Miss.: mansion **135**
Peacock, Gordon **167**
Pelicans **78**, 137, **140-141**
Pictured Rocks National Lakeshore,
Mich. 95, **100**; "Log Slide" area **104**
Pine Ridge Indian Reservation, S.
Dak. 86; ceremonial chief **89**
Ponca Photography Workshop **158**
Porcupine Mountains Wilderness
State Park, Mich. 95, **96, 97**
Prairie dogs **4, 81, 85**
Prairies: agriculture **62-63**, 71, **72-73**,
86-88, 125, livestock 64, 65, **70**, 78,
79, *86;* conservationists 78, 88;
erosion *see* Badlands; festivals **68-
69**; history 62, 64, 65, 70-71, *72*, 78,
79, 87, 88; map **65**; mixed-grass 78,
87; pothole marshes **72-79**; ranches
65, *66, 69*, 71, 78, 79, 86-87;
shortgrass 78, 79; tallgrass 78, 88;
way of life 64, *69*, 70-71, 86, 87; wild
flowers 64, 65, 78, **84, 85**, 88;
wildlife **4**, 65, 78, **81**, 85-86, **86, 90-
91**, birds *72, 74,* **75, 77-81, 84**
Presque Isle Park, Mich. **101**
Presque Isle River, Mich. **96**
Pronghorns 85, **86**
Pueblo Bonito, N. Mex. 188
Pueblo Indians 180, *184*, 188 *see also*
Hopi Indians; ancestors *see* Anasazi

Randolph, Vance 146, 165
Rappelling **16**, 19
Raymond, Nick **83**
Red Mountain, Colo. 180
Reese River Valley, Nev. 26-27
Richards, Jack 157, 164
Rock art, Indian 19, 188, 189, **191**
Rollenhagen, Dick 99
Roosevelt, Theodore 65; quoted *66*

St. François Mountains, Mo. 156
St. Martinville, La.: park **122-123**
Sakakawea, Lake, N. Dak. 87
San Juan Mission: Utah 189-191
San Juan Mountains, Colo. 172-173,
174-178; minerals 179; railroad
178, 179
San Juan River, U. S. 189, 190
Sand Hills, Nebr. 87
Sand paintings 180-181, **182, 183**
Sanibel Island, Fla. 136-137
Schiller, Elizabeth Lloyd **57**; home 55,
56-57, 58
Schools **23**, 43, 70, 87, **157, 169**
Seafood **34-35**, 36, *37,* **40-41**, **128-129**,

136; cooking *39*, 43, **49**, 58, 59;
festivals **38-39, 49**; harvesting **34-35**,
44-46, 54, 55
Sellers, Gerard 133
Sheep: bighorn sheep 11, 78; ranches
21, 27, 79, **176-177**
Ship Rock (pinnacle), N. Mex. 180,
181
Shipwrecks 111, 118
Shoshone Indians 10; village 11, **12**,
18
Sigsbee (skipjack) **44-45**, 54, 55
Silver 118, 179, 181, *187*, 188; mines *6*,
20, 25, 172, 179, 180
Sioux Indians 64; Oglala Sioux 86, **89**
Smith, John: quoted 36
Smith Island, Md. 36-37, **40-41**, 43,
48, 49; churches 42-43, **43**
South Dakota: badlands 79, **82-83**, 85,
86, **90-91**; dinosaur fossils 79; gold
mining 79; national parks **4-5, 82-
83**, 85, 86; prairies 64, 70, *72*, 85;
sod house **71**
Stilwell, Okla.: school **157**
Strubel family 165, 166
Superior, Lake, Canada-U. S. 94-95,
96, 99, 104, 111, 112, *113*
Sybrant, Austin, and family 87

Tahquamenon Falls, Mich. 112
Tangier Island, Va. 36-37, 42, 49;
houses 42, **58-61**; watermen **34-35**
Taylor Canyon, Nev. 196
Teche, Bayou, La. *123*, **128-129**
Telluride, Colo. *6*, **174-175**, 179, 180
Ten Thousand Islands, Fla.:
mangrove islands 137, **140-143**
Texas: beaches **116-117**, 118, **120**;
cowboy **116**; storms 118, 119, 124
Theaters 28, **29**, 71
Theodore Roosevelt National Park, N.
Dak. 65, **66-67**, 70
Thimbleberries 98, **98**
Thomas, David Hurst 11
Thomas, Joshua 42
Trains 70-71, **178, 179**
Traiteur (healer) 126, 133
Trapping 20, 70, 125, 133, 156
Trotter, Pearl 64
Trotters, N. Dak.: sole resident **68**
Turquoise **18**, 26, 111, 181; mines **18**,
25, 26
Tylerton, Md. **40-41**, 43, **43**, 48

Upper Peninsula, Mich.: area 94;
economic hardship 94, *95*, 98-99,
104, 113; ethnic diversity 95, *95*,
105; festivals 105, **108, 109**; forests
94, **97**, 98, 99, **100**, *104*, 105, **106-
107**, 112, 113; history 98, 104, 105,
111; loggers and logging *95*, 104,

105, **109**, 112, 113; maps 94, **95;**
museums 99, 111; natural history
104, 112; parks 95, **96, 97**, 99, **100**,
101, 104; record snowfall 99; resorts
98, 111-112, **114-115;** sportfishing
102-103, 112, 113; way of life *92*, 94,
99, 104, 105, *111*, 113; wildlife *96*,
98, **102**, 112, 113
Urbanna, Va.: oyster festival **49**
Utah: national parks **170-171**, 191;
religious communities 20, *22*, **22-23**,
172, 189-191; rock art **191**; rock
formations **170-171**, 190, 191, **192-
195**

Veeser, William L. 99
Voelker, John *102*, **103**, 112, 113

Wahpeton Prairie, Minn. 88
Walnut Grove School, Ark. **169**
Waterfalls **7**, 112, **149, 159**, 179-180
Watermen **34-35**, 36, *39*, **40**, 42, 43,
44-46, 48, 49, 54, 55, 58, 59
Wheatfields **62-63**, 64, 78
Whitaker, James, and family **161**
White Pine, Mich.: copper 99
"wickiup" 11, **12**
Wild flowers 98, 112; badlands **66-67**,
85; prairies 64, 65, 78, **84**, 85, **85**, 88
Wilder, Laura Ingalls 88
Willey, Guy 53-54
Wilson Mesa, Colo. **176-177**
Wind Cave National Park, S. Dak. **4-5**
Wind-surfing **121**
Wood carvings **154, 155, 186**; decoys
48, 59
Woodworking 165-166
Wye House, near Easton, Md. 55, **56-
57,** 58

Yoopers 94, *95*, 113

Zinc 156, 179

Library of Congress CIP Data
Main entry under title:

America's hidden corners.

1. United States—Description
and travel—1981- —Addresses,
essays, lectures.   I. National
Geographic Society (U. S.).   Special
Publications Division.
E169.04.A53 1983 917.3'04927
82-47844

ISBN 0-87044-441-7 (regular
binding)
ISBN 0-87044-446-8 (library
binding)

Composition for *America's Hidden Corners* by National Geographic's Photographic
Services, Carl M. Shrader, Director, Lawrence F. Ludwig, Assistant Director. Printed and bound by Holladay-Tyler Printing Corp., Rockville, Md. Color separations
by the Lanman Progressive Co., Washington, D. C.; Lincoln Graphics, Inc., Cherry
Hill, N.J.; NEC, Inc., Nashville, Tenn.